SEMINAR STUDIES IN HISTORY

Editor: Patrick Richardson

ELIZABETHAN
IRELAND

SEMINAR STUDIES IN HISTORY

Editor: Patrick Richardson

A full list of titles in this
series will be found on the
back cover of this book

SEMINAR STUDIES IN HISTORY

ELIZABETHAN IRELAND

Grenfell Morton

Lecturer in History
Department of Extra-Mural Studies
The Queen's University of Belfast

LONGMAN

LONGMAN GROUP LIMITED
London

*Associated companies, branches and representatives
throughout the world*

© Longman Group Ltd 1971

First published 1971

ISBN 0582 31423 2

PRINTED IN GREAT BRITAIN BY
WESTERN PRINTING SERVICES LTD, BRISTOL

Contents

Maps

Introduction to the Series

The seminar method of teaching is being used increasingly in VI forms and at universities. It is a way of learning in smaller groups through discussion, designed both to get away from and to supplement the basic lecture techniques. To be successful, the members of a seminar must be informed, or else—in the unkind phrase of a cynic—it can be a 'pooling of ignorance'. The chapter in the textbook of English or European history by its nature cannot provide material in this depth, but at the same time the full academic work may be too long and perhaps too advanced for students at this level.

For this reason we have invited practising teachers in universities, schools and colleges of further education to contribute short studies on specialised aspects of British and European history with these special needs and pupils of this age in mind. For this series the authors have been asked to provide, in addition to their basic analysis, a full selection of documentary material of all kinds and an up-to-date and comprehensive bibliography. Both these sections are referred to in the text, but it is hoped that they will prove to be valuable teaching and learning aids in themselves.

Note on the System of References:

A bold number in round brackets (**5**) in the text refers the reader to the corresponding entry in the Bibliography section at the end of the book.

A bold number in square brackets, preceded by 'doc.' [**docs 6, 8**] refers the reader to the corresponding items in the section of Documents, which follows the main text.

PATRICK RICHARDSON
General Editor

Acknowledgements

I am indebted to the late Professor Edmund Curtis, Trinity College, Dublin, and to the late Mrs Margaret O'Callaghan, also of Dublin, for laying the foundation of my interest in Irish history; to Professors T. W. Moody and Jocelyn Otway-Ruthven, and the late Constantia Maxwell, of Trinity College, Dublin, for their stimulating teaching; to my colleagues F. J. Whitford, J. Frey and Dr L. Muinzer, of the Department of Extra-Mural Studies, Queen's University, Belfast, for enlarging my understanding of Irish history; to B. C. S. Wilson, of the Department of Archaeology, Queen's University, for sharing in the exploration of local history; and to my students in Belfast, Coleraine and Dungannon, for their patience and tolerance.

Particular thanks are due to Mr James Bolton, of the Department of Education, Queen's University, and Mr David Kennedy, President of the Ulster Society for Irish Historical Studies, both of whom read the MS and made many helpful suggestions; also to Mrs Lis Paton, now of Sarnia, Ontario, who prepared the typescript, and to Mr Peter Paton, who carefully checked it for me. I am also grateful to Mrs Joan Kenny for her expert cartographical advice.

Finally, my wife deserves much thanks for being such a patient listener and constructive critic.

G. M.

We are grateful to the following for permission to reproduce copyright material:

George Allen & Unwin Ltd. for the extracts from *Irish History From Contemporary Sources* by Constantia Maxwell; The Cambridge University Press for the extracts from *The Voyages and Colonising Enterprises of Sir Humphrey Gilbert, Vol. 1* by D. B. Quinn; and Methuen & Co. Ltd. for the extracts from *Irish Historical Documents* edited by E. Curtis and R. B. McDowell.

We have been unable to trace the copyright holder of *Captain Cuellar's Adventures in Connacht and Ulster* and *Captain Cuellar's Narra-*

tive of the Spanish Armada and his Adventures in Ireland by H. Allingham, translated by R. Crawford, and would appreciate any information that would enable us to do so.

The cover photograph is taken from *Pacata Hibernia* by T. Stafford.

The plan of Kinsale on page 94 is based on the map in *Pacata Hibernia* by T. Stafford with additional details from maps in *Mountjoy* by F. M. Jones and *Irish Battles* by G. A. Hayes-McCoy.

Part One

BACKGROUND

1 Introduction

EUDOXUS: But if that country of Ireland, whence you lately came, be of so good and commodious a soil, as you report, I wonder that no course is taken for the turning thereof to good use, and reducing that nation to better government and civility.

EDMUND SPENSER, *A View of the State of Ireland* (in **21**)

Elizabeth I was faced with many difficulties on her accession to the throne in 1558, and among these the condition of Ireland proved to be most complex. The situation in that island had evolved over several centuries, presenting a problem which was destined to be a constant factor of Elizabeth's reign, not indeed to be resolved until after her death.

Ireland was, like Scotland, a poor country on the western edge of Europe. It had never enjoyed a strong central government, as had England since the eleventh century; overmighty subjects lorded it over vast tracts of the country; large areas had either never been made subject to English law or had reverted to Gaelic rule during the long decline of English influence in the fourteenth and fifteenth centuries. These factors were exacerbated by the divisive effects of the religious changes introduced under Henry VIII. In its turn the Reformation placed Ireland firmly on the chessboard of European power politics, making Spanish intervention in Irish affairs mirror English interest in the revolt of the Netherlands (**2, 5**).

Under Elizabeth the slow process of conquering the unsubdued areas was completed, the powerful Gaelic and Anglo-Irish lordships were brought to an end, and there was a steady growth in the effective power of the Dublin government. By 1603 the whole of Ireland had been brought for the first time under the authority of a central government, and English law and administration were supreme. In addition the official religion was Anglican, as in England and Wales, even though the majority of the population remained faithful to the older dispensation. The lengthy process of extending English influence in Ireland by arrangement or by confiscation culminated in the plantation of Ulster under James I, an event which marked the transition to modern times (**1, 12**).

WEAKNESS OF THE CENTRAL GOVERNMENT

In England, Elizabeth succeeded to the Crown of a country which had normally enjoyed the benefits of a strong central government since the Norman Conquest. In Ireland this was not so. The Lordship of Ireland, which had been granted to Henry II by Pope Adrian II in the Bull 'Laudabiliter', had never been fully achieved in practice (**16**). The Normans were few in number, they intermarried from the start with the native Irish stock, they adopted the Irish language and Irish laws and customs, and many of the greatest estates came to be held by absentees or minors. The monarch, too, was an absentee, and although visits by Henry II, John or Richard II, created a stir at the time, they did little to maintain a continuously effective central authority (**5**). Further, there were large areas, such as Ulster west of Lough Neagh, where the Normans had never penetrated, and other areas, for instance Connacht, where the new lords of the soil were rapidly absorbed and became more Irish than the Irish themselves. Indeed, by 1270 the failure of the Norman Conquest in Ireland had become apparent (**3, 5**).

The devastating invasion of Edward Bruce in 1315–18, and the murder of William de Burgo, the Earl of Ulster in 1333, introduced two centuries marked, as elsewhere in western Europe, by the decay of central authority and the rise of local lordships (**2**). The statutes of Kilkenny in 1366 endeavoured to conserve what was left of English manners and customs by introducing what amounted to a system of apartheid. For example, intermarriage between English and Irish was forbidden, trade was restricted and a clear distinction drawn between the clergy of the two races. Even riding a horse in the Irish fashion, without a proper saddle, was made unlawful for English subjects. The logical consequence of these statutes was the definition of an area under English law known as the 'land of peace', that is, the territory under the King's peace, as opposed to areas under march law, and Gaelic areas under brehon law (**3, 16**). In the mid-fourteenth century the counties and liberties of Louth, Meath, Trim, Dublin, Kildare, Kilkenny, Wexford, Waterford and Tipperary were listed as being in the King's peace; by 1395 this 'English land' had shrunk to the territory east of a line from Dundalk to Trim and Waterford (**5**). This was the 'Pale', marked off from the rest of Ireland by a ditch and palisade. This was sound policy,

Sixteenth Century Ireland

KINTYRE

GALLOWAY

(O'Doherty)

Lough Foyle

ROUTE

GLENS OF
ANTRIM

Lough Swilly

DERRY

Derry

(O'Cahan)

R. Bann

TYRCONNELL
(O'Donnell)

TYRONE
(O'Neill)

Larne

Carrickfergus

(Mac Sweeny)

Lough
Erne

ULSTER

CLANDEBOY
(O'Neill)

Killybegs

Ballyshannon

Lough Neagh

FERMANAGH
(Maguire)

Armagh

Sligo

BREFNI
(O'Rourke)

MONAGHAN
(MacMahon)

MAYO
(Burke)

CAVAN
((O'Reilly)

Carlingford

Dundalk

CONNACHT

LOUTH

MEATH

Drogheda

GALWAY
(Clanrickard
Burke)

R. Shannon

Trim

THE PALE

Galway

KING'S
COUNTY
(O'Connor)

Maynooth

Dublin

KILDARE

THOMOND
(O'Brien)

Maryborough

WICKLOW
(O'Byrne/O'Toole)

LEINSTER

ORMOND
(Butler)

QUEEN'S COUNTY
(O'More)

Limerick

Kilkenny

Tipperary

MUNSTER

Wexford

Waterford

Dungarvan

Dingle

KERRY

DESMOND
(Fitzgerald)

DECIES

PEMBROKE-
SHIRE

Cork

Youghal

(O'Sullivan)

MUSKERRY
(MacCarthy)

Kinsale

0   30   60 Miles

for this 'eastern triangle' was easy to hold, enjoyed good communications with England and Wales, and provided a base for expeditions into the central plain of Ireland (**2**). In 1465 the Pale had shrunk to its smallest size, including only the four home counties of Dublin, Kildare, Meath and Louth. Even in this small area the use of the Gaelic language was becoming common, and the inhabitants had much cause to complain of extortion and misgovernment (**17**, pp. 82–5).

Dublin, 'the royal city of Ireland, its most noble mart and chief seat of justice', was the seat of the administration. The monarch was represented by the Lord Deputy, who was advised by a council of state. He was empowered to grant pardons under the Great Seal of Ireland, treasons against the person of the monarch being excepted. He was responsible for the armed forces, and could call for a general levy or 'hosting' of the 'Englishry' of the Pale. In short, as the representative of the Crown the Lord Deputy could do all things of regal authority save coining of money. Occasionally he received the more honorific title of Lord Lieutenant, and, on the death of a Lord Deputy, it was the usual custom to appoint one or more Lords Justices to represent the Crown (**17**, pp. 355, 383–4).

The courts of King's Bench, Common Pleas, Exchequer and Chancery were all in the capital, together with the office of the Master of the Rolls. 'And all causes in these several courts were pleaded in the English tongue, and after the manner of the courts in London, save that Ireland of old times had made such frequent relapses to the sword, as the practice of the law was often discontinued, and the custom of the courts by intermission were many times forgotten, and the places being then of small profit were often supplied by unlearned and unpractised men' (**17**, pp. 382–4). The Irish parliament was seldom summoned. It had little significance as an instrument for raising revenue, for during the sixteenth century the ordinary or hereditary revenue was sufficient for the costs of the civil administration. It did not represent all the communities of the realm, but only those counties and towns under English law, and consequently reflected the views of the Anglo-Irish colony in Ireland. In England ten parliaments met during Elizabeth's reign, while in Ireland only three were summoned: in 1560, 1569–70 and 1585–6 (**108**).

TOWNS AND TRADE

Dublin, as the capital of the kingdom of Ireland, was sometimes called the 'Irish' or 'Young' London. It was a walled town, 'defended also on the south with ramparts, having six gates, which open into suburbs'. These walls were an essential defence against the O'Byrnes and the O'Tooles whose fastnesses in the Wicklow hills lay but a few miles to the southward. On their account, 'the city is constrained to keep strong watch lest on a sudden these rebels that lurk in these mountains do set the suburbs on fire'. Within the walls lay the impressive pile of the castle, 'a royal castle fortified with ditches, towers and a magazine built about the year 1220 . . .'. There were two cathedrals, Christ Church and St Patrick's, to remind the citizens of the Norse and Norman founders of their city, some fine parish churches and the monastery of All Hallows, lying to the east of the city. Near Christ Church was the Town Hall, 'where the Mayor hears causes, and where the assemblies of the citizens are held'.

As might have been expected prices in Dublin were higher than elsewhere in Ireland. The presence of a large official class, with all their 'servants, friends and followers . . . maketh the citizens to raise their prices in all things'. But it also meant that there was a ready market for silk, fine cloths, satin, spices, wines and other luxuries 'that would never be vended among the Irish themselves' (**17,** pp. 354–9). Dublin's trade was mainly with London, Bristol and Chester, and her merchant class included some very wealthy men whose shops were 'replenished with all sorts of wares, as well mercery, as grocery, and drapery, both linen and woollen, and there is neither silk man nor milliner in London, that can show better wares'.

Dundalk and Drogheda were the two other towns of significance in the Pale. During the sixteenth century they grew in importance, exporting vast quantities of yarn, wool fells and tallow. Their rise indicated the increasing growth of a maritime economy bordering the Irish Sea, and the increasing influence of Tudor mercantilism over the Irish economy (**33**).

From Dundalk right round to Galway in the west there were no towns of any importance. At Carlingford and at Carrickfergus there were small harbours and some merchants' houses close by the massive grey piles of the Norman castles, while in such havens as

Olderfleet (Larne harbour), Loughs Foyle and Swilly, Mulroy Bay, Killybegs harbour and the anchorage of Ballyshannon, vessels could find shelter and exchange cargoes of wine, salt and iron, to say nothing of muskets and powder, for fish, salted hides (including the pelts of otter, marten and wolf), and wool.

Galway's nearest rival was Limerick on the Shannon estuary. Limerick had a rich agricultural hinterland to draw on, and exported much wheat and barley. It was built on an island, the river being so navigable that a ship of 200 tons could sail right up to the quays of the town. The town itself was divided into two parts: 'that called the upper town in which are the cathedral and the castle, has two gates with handsome stone bridges with battlements and draw-bridges, one leading westward, the other eastward, to which last below adjoins a town walled round with its castle and outworks' (**17**, p. 370). It was noted that along the western coast from the bays of Donegal to the Shannon that 'Spaniards and Bretons have the trade, and few or no Englishmen come there, but only to Galway. And likewise from Limerick to Cork, the Spaniards and Bretons have the trade, as well of the fishings there, as of buying their hides, which is the greatest merchandise of this land, and furnish Irishmen upon that south coast of Munster with salt, iron, guns and powder.' Cork, 'happily planted on the sea' had a magnificent natural harbour, and was looked upon as the fourth town in Ireland. It formed a contrast to smaller port towns such as Dingle, Kinsale, Dungarvan, Ross, Youghal and Wexford, all of which declined in importance during the sixteenth century. Ross became 'a poor, ruined town', and Kinsale was destined to be by 1603 'a poor town ruined by the late rebellion'. Finally, the *urbs intacta*, Waterford, owed its impor-tance to the route across the Irish Sea from Milford Haven, although Bristol and Chester had now eclipsed that port in the Irish Trade. The town was 'properly builded and very well compact, somewhat close by reason of their thick buildings and narrow streets'. There were nearly a thousand houses, surrounded by 'a stone wall, some-thing less than a mile in circumference with seventeen towers. . . . It is the richest town in Ireland after Dublin, and vessels of from 300–400 tons lie at the quays . . . the trade of the port is with Galicia, Portugal, Andalusia, and Biscay, where they send fish, hides, salt, meat, and at times wheat and barley' (**17**, pp. 368, 372–4, 362–4).

GAELIC SOCIETY

The majority of Irishmen lived in a pastoral economy, exchanging goods through barter. This essentially peasant economy proved to be surprisingly resilient, and did not finally collapse until after the Great Famine of the 1840s. Wealth was reckoned in herds of cattle and brood mares. These herds, known as 'creaghts', moved from the plains to their summer pastures in the hills. This custom of transhumance or 'booleying' led some English observers to conclude that the Gaelic septs were nomadic. However, these seasonal movements took place within well-defined territories, although cattle-raiding frequently took place as a means of exacting tribute or impoverishing enemies (**14**).

The majority of the people were unfree, thought of contemptuously as 'churls' by those who were free. Of these the majority were landed freeholders, the minority being the brehon lawyers, the poets and chroniclers, the skilled craftsmen and, in some areas, the gallowglasses or mercenary soldiers, who were allotted lands in return for military services. The landed freeholders were grouped together under a chieftain, lord, captain or 'ri' (king), in an area of about 300–400 square miles known as a 'tuath'. In each tuath the chieftain was selected from the kinship group, or 'derbfine', of the ruling family by an assembly of the freemen. To provide for the succession of some suitable male, and to prevent the perils of minorities, the chieftain's successor or 'tanist' was nominated from amongst the 'derbfine' during the lifetime of the incumbent. This institution of tanistry was meant to provide for an orderly succession, but in fact it frequently led instead to disorder and murder. When the time came for the inauguration of the chief the freemen of the sept assembled at their traditional crowning-place and there the chief was acclaimed by his title: The O'Neill, The Maguire or The MacMurrough Kavanagh, for example [**doc. 17**].

Elizabethan observers found this principle of succession by tanistry hard to grasp, as it formed such a contrast to the principle of primogeniture, with its rule of succession to property from father to first-born son, or the nearest male or female heir. A related point was the difference in English and Irish law about the ownership of land. Under brehon law the territory of the sept belonged not to individuals or to the chief *in propria persona*, but to the freemen of the whole

9

group. True, some land was allotted to the chieftain as demesne, but this did not affect the fact that he was not a landlord in the English sense. The freeholders held their land for a certain length of time only, as it was periodically redistributed among the members of the kinship group within the sept on a principle which appeared to English legal observers to be similar to that of gavelkind (**17**, pp. 330–1). If the chieftain rebelled, and suffered confiscation not only of his own mensal lands, but of the sept lands, it is not surprising that the members of the sept legitimately felt this as a burning grievance, as their lands were swept away by what was to them an alien and indefensible law. Indeed, this conflict of two differing legal systems lay at the root of the clash of the Tudor and Gaelic civilisations [**doc. 5**].

Each Gaelic chieftain maintained himself, and his train of soldiers and camp-followers, by quartering himself in different households in his territory, and enjoying free hospitality as long as supplies held out. This was called 'coshering', and was an essential part of the basic principle of this pre-feudal society: 'spend me and defend me'. Coshering symbolised the relation of clientship between chief and free landholder; it also supplemented the real income which the lords derived from their own demesne lands in the tuath. The other 'cuttings and spendings' claimed by the lords included 'bonaght', which was a levy for the upkeep of the soldiers; 'coyne and livery', which meant the provision of food and lodging for men and horses; and 'cess' which can be thought of as a localised form of benevolence or forced loan. These exactions were frequently arbitrary and oppressive [**doc. 2**]. When English law replaced brehon law, and the chieftain became a landlord, as in the 'composition' of Connacht in 1585, or in the settlement of Monaghan in 1591, the ordinary tenants welcomed the definition of their rents and the limitations thus placed on the fiscal exactions of their former chieftain.

The tuath was the basic unit of Gaelic society, although it usually formed a part of a larger grouping under the rule of an important family group. For instance, the O'Cahans were lords of much of modern co. Derry, the MacMahons of Monaghan. the O'Reillys of Cavan or the O'Sullivans of west Cork. These lords in their turn ranked as 'urraghts', or subkings, under the supremacy of greater lords who were in effect provincial kings. Such were the O'Donnells in Tyrconnell (Donegal), who looked on the O'Dohertys, the MacSweeneys and the Maguires as their urraghts; the family of

MacCarthy More in Cork, who claimed tribute from their collaterals, the septs of MacCarthy Reagh and MacCarthy Muskerry, and from the O'Sullivans; and, finally, the great O'Neills of Tyrone in Ulster, who claimed supremacy over the O'Cahans, the O'Hanlons and the MacMahons, and who regarded themselves as a cut above the O'Donnells and the lesser O'Neills of Clandeboy (north Down and south Antrim). These lordships were not clan territories in the Scottish sense; Monaghan was not, for example, populated exclusively by persons bearing the surname MacMahon, any more than Brefni (the modern counties of Leitrim and Cavan) was entirely filled with O'Rourkes and O'Reillys (**21, 61, 62,** and see map 1).

THE ANGLO-IRISH LORDSHIPS

The Anglo-Irish lords occupied the middle band of the spectrum between the Pale on the one hand, and the independent Gaelic chieftains on the other. Their position on the spectrum was determined by their degree of hibernicisation. Those who had adopted Gaelic dress and brehon law were known as 'degenerate English' to distinguish them from the 'mere' (unmixed or native) Irish. Such were the former de Burgos of Connacht, who had become the gaelicised MacWilliam Burkes of Mayo and Clanrickard Burkes of Galway, and the Mandevilles of the Route (in north Antrim) who had evolved into MacQuillans, and who, in the sixteenth century, were looked upon as being of Welsh descent (**3, 59**).

Two Anglo-Irish families were of outstanding importance: the Fitzgeralds and the Butlers. The Fitzgeralds or Geraldines were descended from Maurice Fitzgerald, one of the Norman knights who had come to Ireland with 'Strongbow' (Richard Fitzgilbert, Earl of Pembroke), and were proud of their supposed family connection with the Gherardhini of Florence (**21,** appendix, 431–5). They were divided into two main branches: the house of Desmond and the house of Kildare. In the early fourteenth century Maurice Fitzthomas was created Earl of Desmond. His lands included Cork, the district known as the Decies in west Waterford, Kerry, where he was granted a palatine jurisdiction [**doc. 10**], and Limerick, which contained his chief castles at Askeaton and Shanid (**72**). Under the supremacy of the Earls of Desmond were such lesser Geraldines as the Knight of Glin, and the White Knight of Kilmallock (**58**), and even the

Background

MacCarthy's of Carbery and Muskerry in west Cork, who were important Gaelic chieftains in their own right. The Desmonds intermarried with the princely O'Briens of Thomond (Clare) and, in defiance of the statutes of Kilkenny, took all the customary Irish exactions of 'coign and livery, cartings, lodgings, cosherings, bonnaught and such like', privileges which notably supplemented their income, and placed the Desmonds on a par with the proudest overmighty subject in Tudor England (**55, 56**).

The Earl of Desmond was appointed Lord Deputy in 1463, and unwisely paraded his alliances with Gaelic society outside the 'King's peace'. His downfall was swift and surprising. At a meeting of the Irish parliament at Drogheda in 1467 Desmond was attainted for 'horrible treasons and felonies', and was subsequently beheaded. This deed had the result of ensuring the disloyalty of the house of Desmond, and foreshadowed its extinction in 1583.

The Wars of the Roses in England created conditions in which some form of aristocratic home rule became inevitable in Ireland, and so real power passed to the other branch of the Geraldines: the house of Kildare. In 1470 Thomas, Earl of Kildare, became justiciar. Under his son Gerald Fitzgerald, the eighth earl, who became Lord Deputy in 1477, the supremacy of the Anglo-Irish aristocracy reached its height (**54**). Gerald (who was nicknamed Garret More) allied himself with the great O'Neills of Tyrone by his sister's marriage to Con O'Neill in 1480, and further strengthened his position by the marriage of his daughters to Ulick Burke of Clanrickard in Galway, Donal MacCarthy Reagh in Cork and Sir Piers Butler. This latter match may have been designed to alleviate the Montague and Capulet hostility of the Geraldines and the Butlers:

> Two households, both alike in dignity,
>
> . . .
>
> From ancient grudge break to new mutiny,
> Where civil blood makes civil hands unclean.
> (W. Shakespeare, *Romeo and Juliet*, prologue)

The Butlers were descended from Theobald Walter, who had been appointed Butler of Ireland by King John, and had subsequently obtained large grants of land in Kilkenny and Tipperary, part of which was erected into a palatine jurisdiction [**doc. 10**]. The Butlers took their title of Ormond from these lands in eastern Munster.

Their fiefs formed a solid block separating the Geraldine lands in Desmond from those in Kildare, and squabbles over lordship and tribute were therefore inevitable.

To make matters worse the Butlers supported the Lancastrians, whereas most of the Anglo-Irish magnates, largely influenced by the Geraldines, were firmly Yorkist. James, fifth Earl of Ormond, was executed after the battle of Towton in England in 1461, and in 1462 his brother John Butler was defeated at Pilltown in Tipperary by the Earl of Desmond. Such events only served to increase the bitter rivalry of the Butlers and the Geraldines, and to underline the pro-English tendencies of the Butlers (3).

2 The Revival of Royal Authority

'Tir mharbh tir gan tighearna' (a land without a lord is a dead land).

Maxim of the Irish brehon lawyers

POYNINGS' LAW

The victory of Bosworth marked the end of the strife in England, and the accession of Henry VII began that 'Tudor despotism' which led to the downfall of overmighty subjects in England and eventually in Ireland (**7, 53**). The cautious Henry, always a realist in politics, knew that nothing could be done to replace Garret More, the overmighty Earl of Kildare, as Lord Deputy so long as it remained true that, 'since all Ireland cannot rule this man, this man must rule all Ireland'.

It was a crafty move to enlist the house of Kildare on the royal side, for it invested the King's lordship over Ireland with the real wealth and resources of the earldom. Nevertheless, Henry was determined to curb the powers of the Irish Parliament, which had become an instrument in the hands of the Anglo-Irish lords. Sir Edward Poynings was appointed Lord Deputy, and he summoned a meeting of Parliament at Drogheda in 1494. An Act was passed—known subsequently as Poynings' Law—which provided, in brief, that no Bills should come before the Irish parliament unless they had first been approved by both the Irish and English Privy Councils [**doc. 6**]. This effectively muzzled the legislative initiative of the Irish parliament, although, in Elizabeth's reign, it came to be regarded by the Anglo-Irish as a safeguard against measures being rushed through parliament by the Lord Deputy and the council in Dublin. Though few people paid much attention to it at the time, Poynings' Law was a reassertion of English sovereignty in Ireland, a sovereignty which was to cover the entire island by 1603. It also asserted the inferiority of the Irish legislature, something which was not to be questioned until the end of the seventeenth century (**16, 108, 95, 53**). The Act itself was not repealed until Grattan's time in 1782.

On Poynings's departure in January 1496 Henry VII again appointed the Earl of Kildare as Lord Deputy. Kildare behaved like an uncrowned king. The Guild of St George, with its military panoply, followed his summons in the Pale, as did his feudatories and kinsmen. At the battle of Knocktoe in Galway in 1504 Kildare defeated the Clanrickard Burkes and entered the town of Galway in triumph (**41**). Finally, the great Earl was shot dead in 1513 during a skirmish on the frontiers of the Pale with some of the O'Mores of Leix. He was succeeded as Earl of Kildare and as Lord Deputy by his son Garret Oge. Times, however, had changed and Garret Oge found his splendid position being gradually eroded. He was opposed by Cardinal Wolsey, by the growing body of English government officials in the Dublin administration, and by his enemy Sir Piers Butler. Further, after 1519 Henry VIII began to take an active interest in Irish affairs. Henry wished to 'devise howe Ireland may be reduced and restored to good order and obedience' (**117**). A detailed and optimistic policy of 'sober ways, politic drifts and amiable persuasions' was introduced [**doc. 7**]. By this it was hoped to revive the loyalty of the great Anglo-Irish lords, to recall outlying lands such as those of Connacht and parts of Munster to obedience, to extend the King's peace, to establish a proper collection of taxes over the whole country, to unify and anglicise the church, and to introduce more of the English by birth (as opposed to the Anglo-Irish or 'English by descent') into the government and administration. This last provision was most important (**17**, pp. 103–5). The reconstruction of the Privy Council by the introduction of such men as the Archbishop of Dublin, Brabazon, the Treasurer of War, and John Alen, Master of the Rolls, brought that body firmly under the control of Henry's 'new men'. This small beginning marked a new approach to Irish affairs, and indicated that the day of Anglo-Irish ascendancy in the administration had ended.

The year 1534 was a turning-point in Irish history. By then it had become clear that a continuous policy of intervention by the Crown had begun, and the opportunity to implement this policy still further was provided by the fall of the house of Kildare. Garret Oge had never recovered from wounds he had sustained in a skirmish in 1532, and his position had been slowly undermined by his numerous enemies for some years. In 1534 he was summoned to London, and placed in the Tower on a charge of treasonable activity. His son 'Silken Thomas' (Thomas Fitzgerald, Lord Offaly), stung by the false report of his father's death, flew into rebellion. He resigned his commission from the Crown, and attacked the outskirts of Dublin.

However, the rebellion of Silken Thomas was shortlived. Maynooth castle was taken in March 1535, and the garrison put to the sword after the surrender, 'for the dread and example of others'. This notorious 'Pardon of Maynooth' indicated the ruthlessness of the Tudors, and struck a note in Irish warfare which became commonplace under Elizabeth (**116, 117, 17**, pp. 96–7 [cf. **doc. 20**]).

Silken Thomas was placed under the ban of the Church, a ban so severe that his father, Garret Oge, died in the Tower on reading it. Finally, Silken Thomas was executed at Tyburn in 1537, together with five of his uncles. So ended the power of the Geraldines of the house of Kildare.

REFORMATION CHANGES IN IRELAND

The measures passed by the Reformation parliament in England, 1529–36, had in sum led to the replacement of papal by royal supremacy over the Church in England. It was therefore inevitable that Henry VIII should extend similar measures to Ireland now that the way seemed clear for the re-establishment of the authority of the Crown in that country (**9**). A parliament was summoned to meet in Dublin in 1536, and in the following year Henry was declared the 'only supreme head in earth of the whole Church of Ireland'. This was followed by an act against the authority of the Bishop of Rome, and an act against Appeals. All the monasteries in the English Pale, such as Bective, Baltinglass, Holmpatrick, and All Hallows in Dublin, were dissolved, together with those in the Butler lands in Kilkenny and Ormond, and monastic institutions in the towns of Munster (**17**, pp. 126–8). Outside those areas the monasteries continued to function right up to the reign of James I. Nothing indicated more clearly the partial control exercised by the Crown over Ireland, a fact which prevented the enforcement of any kind of uniformity as in England (**16, 50, 51**).

The immediate effect of these changes was to weaken royal prestige in Ireland, even though these changes were not so much doctrinal as in ecclesiastical administration. The ultimate effect was to link the progress of protestantism with the advance of conquest and plantation, so producing a fatal alignment of religious and political attitudes. It must be added that Ireland was unprepared for doctrinal changes, for there had been no *preparatio evangelica* as there had been in Germany before Luther's time, or as in England in the days of Wycliffe.

It has been pointed out that, 'of the Bishops in office at the passing of the Reformation legislation under Henry VIII, six (or at most eight) accepted the new spiritual allegiance, while twenty-one continued in communion with Rome' (**50**). Henry, however, could not pursue contradictory policies in England and Ireland. Yet the religious changes made the Tudor task of reducing Ireland both tedious and complicated, for the tides of the Counter-Reformation inevitably drew Ireland closer to the mainstream of European affairs, and made it impossible for England to avoid becoming increasingly enmeshed in the problems of Ireland. The Counter-Reformation strengthened Irish links with catholic Europe, and particularly with Spain. Fishing and trading vessels brought priests to and fro, and in 1542 the first Jesuit mission to Ireland was appointed (**17**, pp. 146–50). Such emissaries found their task made all the easier by the inadequacy of the reformed Church, many of whose clergy shared the widespread ignorance about Ireland, who made no effort for over a century to preach in the vernacular (Irish), and who, in any event, were themselves but poorly provided for [**doc. 16**]. By 1560, when the Irish parliament passed the Acts of Supremacy and Uniformity which brought the Elizabethan church compromise to Ireland, the battle was over. The majority of Irishmen were firmly on the catholic side, and the official religion of the state and its officials was protestant. It was as decisive an outcome of ecclesiastical affairs as that reached at the same time in the Scotland of John Knox (**52, 48**).

IRELAND BECOMES A KINGDOM

A change in the royal title was a necessary consequence of the fall of the house of Kildare and of the ecclesiastical changes brought about by parliament. The title *Dominus Hiberniae* (Lord of Ireland) rested on a papal grant to Henry II. This was clearly inappropriate in the new circumstances, and so, by the Act 35 Hen. VIII cap. 1, the title King of Ireland was adopted by the Crown [**doc. 8**]. The Act established Ireland as a kingdom, but also clearly stated the doctrine of the union of the Crowns. The Crown of Ireland was to be 'united and knit to the imperial crown of the realm of England'.

Background

In 1541 it can be said that the kingdom of Ireland provided a legal framework whose reality was to be slowly filled in under Elizabeth and James I. It was not until the end of the seventeenth century that the constitutional problems implicit in this Act began to be discussed in Ireland. Indeed the problems of how to relate two kingdoms and a shared Crown formed the core of the imperial debate in Ireland and the American colonies in the eighteenth century. The American Revolution, and the Act of Union, 1800, which established a United Kingdom of Great Britain and Ireland, provided opposite solutions to the same problem (**16, 17,** pp. 101–3).

Henry VIII as a European prince could only devote a fraction of his energies to Irish affairs, and, having settled his title and reformed the Church he now sought to extend English influence among the Gaelic and hibernicised Anglo-Irish lords by the deceptively attractive policy of 'surrender and re-grant'. This was part of Henry's policy of 'sober ways, politic drifts, and amiable persuasions', and meant that the chiefs would surrender their Gaelic titles and receive a title from the Crown instead. For example, there was a grant to Con O'Neill 'for the term of his life, of the title of Earl of Tyrone, and after his death to his son Matthew . . . and his heirs male forever' (**17**, pp. 108–12). Such a grant was not a simple exchange of new lamps for old. It meant that Con O'Neill as Earl of Tyrone agreed to hold his lands from the Crown, that he accepted the principle of primogeniture, whereby his estates would pass to the firstborn male heir; in short, the acceptance of an English title implied full acceptance of English law and rejection of the native or brehon law [**docs. 5, 7**].

At first the policy of peaceful persuasion appeared to produce results. O'Brien became Earl of Thomond, MacWilliam became Earl of Clanricard, agreement was reached with Manus O'Donnell by which he recognised Henry VIII as his liege lord and king. But 'surrender and re-grant' was not without its critics. It really depended entirely on the cooperation of the grantees with the Crown, a slender basis upon which to place the settlement of the kingdom. Indeed, as early as 1521 the Earl of Surrey had expressed the view that Ireland could only be subjected by a policy of military conquest and plantation [**doc. 25**]. Henry, however, was unable and unwilling to undertake such an enterprise. His finances were too straitened, and instead he hoped that his methods of conciliation would help to improve Irish finances sufficiently to enable the new kingdom to pay for itself, and even produce a surplus. Here in essence was the Tudor dilemma: there was the desire to make Ireland a source of profit to the Crown, coupled with a reluctance to spend sufficient on that full settlement which was a precondition of fiscal viability.

By his policy of 'surrender and re-grant' and the establishment of the kingdom of Ireland, Henry VIII had made it clear that English law would prevail. His conciliatory and statesmanlike policy in Ireland would, it was hoped, serve to bring the people 'from rude, beastly, ignorant, cruel and unruly infidels, to the state of civil, reasonable, patient, humble, and well-governed Christians'. Yet, the consequences of Henry's reign were to be a deepening religious division, with a state church supported by a minority of the population; a realisation that brehon law was too deeply rooted to be overthrown by a handful of new titles; a kingdom which had to be conquered in a long period of rebellion and warfare. Such was the legacy of Henry VIII to his daughters (**117**).

THE POLICY OF PLANTATION BEGUN

A forward policy of confiscation and plantation on a limited scale was forced on the government by the condition of the midland areas of Leix and Offaly, which lay to the west of the Pale. The O'Mores and O'Dempseys of Leix and the O'Connors of Offaly had for some time been held in check by the payment of tribute ('Dubh-cosh' or 'black rent'), but as time went on the lawlessness of this western frontierland became less tolerable. In 1528, for instance, Brian O'Connor had actually taken the Lord Deputy prisoner. Trouble continued and in 1537 the Deputy's forces marched in to parts of Offaly hitherto untouched and captured the castle of Dengen. The garrison received the 'Pardon of Maynooth', and were executed after surrendering. The castle was knocked down, and it was officially suggested that permanent garrisons should be stationed in Leix and Offaly (**121**).

Nothing further was done until the reign of Mary I when instructions were issued for the confiscation and plantation of two-thirds of Leix and Offaly, the third nearest to the river Shannon being reserved to the displaced O'Mores, O'Connors and O'Dempseys. The two territories were made shire-ground: Leix became Queen's County, with its military and administrative centre at

19

Background

Maryborough, and Offaly became King's County with a garrison at Dengen, renamed Philipstown in honour of Mary's consort, Philip II of Spain. English subjects were encouraged to settle there, none of them to sell or lease his land to any Irishman of Irish blood or birth, on pain of forfeiture. Military service was obligatory on all settlers, Irish servants were not permitted, and proper houses were to be erected (**17,** pp. 227–34; **34, 121**).

The net result of the plantation of Leix and Offaly was to be fifty years of merciless border warfare. Yet, confiscation was the logical consequence in law of treason and rebellion against the Crown. The scene was now set for the decisive phase in the conquest and settlement of Ireland. As Sir John Davies, the Attorney-General for Ireland, wrote in 1612:

> But the truth is, the conquest of Ireland was made piece and piece by slow steps and degrees, and by several attempts in several ages. There were sundry revolutions as well of the English fortunes as of the Irish, sometimes one prevailing, sometimes the other, and it was never brought to a full period till His Majesty that now is came to the throne (**24**).

Part Two

MAIN DEVELOPMENTS

3 Shane O'Neill

One demanded merrily why Oneile that last was (sc. Shane)
would not frame himself to speak English? 'What', quoth the
other in a rage, 'thinkest thou that it standeth with Oneile his
honour to writhe his mouth in clattering English?'

RICHARD STANIHURST, *A Plain and Perfect Description of Ireland*,
in Holinshed's *Chronicles* (ed. 1808), vi.6.

The medieval order in Ireland had reached its culmination in 1534,
and since then much of that order had been destroyed and the
foundations laid for the modern colonial period of Irish history (**116**).
There had been a policy of continuous intervention by the Crown
which had resulted in the downfall of the overmighty house of
Kildare, the introduction of the Reformation, the replacement of the
medieval lordship by the modern kingdom of Ireland and the
adoption of a positive policy towards the Gaelic lordships. This
policy had two aspects. On the one hand there was the circum-
spection of Henry VIII's 'sober ways, politic drifts, and amiable
persuasions', which had resulted in the conception of 'surrender and
re-grant', a plan which would, it was hoped, metamorphose the old
Gaelic titles into new English ones subject to English law and custom
[**doc. 7**]. On the other hand the events of the short reigns of Edward
VI and Mary I in Leix and Offaly had indicated that a more ruthless
programme of confiscation and plantation was likely to be pursued in
cases of rebellion and refusal to come over peaceably to acceptance
of English rule.

Elizabeth was not left long in doubt about the vitality of the
Gaelic order. That order was firmly established in Ulster west of the
river Bann and Lough Neagh, an area into which the Normans had
not been able to penetrate. Tyrone was the centre of the power of the
great O'Neills, who since the thirteenth century claimed supremacy
over the O'Cahans of Derry, the MacMahons of Monaghan, and the
lesser O'Neills of the Fews in Armagh. Traditionally the O'Neills
even regarded themselves as superior to the proud O'Donnells, who
were the overlords of Tyrconnell (Donegal), and who claimed some
tribute from Fermanagh and Sligo. Yet in 1541 Manus O'Donnell
had signed an agreement with Sir Anthony St Leger, the Lord
Deputy, by which he recognised Henry VIII as his liege lord,

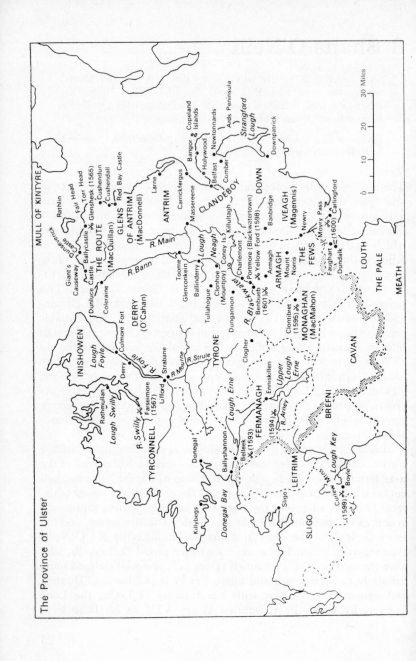

The Province of Ulster

MULL OF KINTYRE

Giant's Causeway
Fair Head
Tor Head
Rathlin
Dunseverick Castle
Dunluce Castle
Ballycastle
Glenshesk (1565)
Cushendun
Cushendall
Red Bay Castle

THE ROUTE (MacQuillan)
GLENS OF ANTRIM (MacDonnell)

Coleraine
Larne
Masereene
Carrickfergus

ANTRIM

Belfast
Holywood
Bangor
Copeland Islands
Newtonnards
Ards Peninsula
Comber
Strangford Lough
Downpatrick

CLANDEBOY
DOWN

R. Main
Killultagh
Banbridge
Newry
IVEAGH (Magennis)
Carlingford
Moyry Pass
(1600)

R. Bann
Toome
Glenconkein
Ballinderry
Clonhoe (Mountjoy)
Coney Is.
Charlemont
Portmore (Blackwatertown)
Yellow Ford (1598)
Armagh
Mount Norris
THE FEWS
Faughart
Dundalk
LOUTH

DERRY (O'Cahan)
Culmore Fort

INISHOWEN
Lough Foyle

Derry
R. Foyle
Strabane
Lifford
R. Mourne
R. Strule
Dungannon
R. Blackwater
Benburb (1601)

TYRONE
Clogher
ARMAGH

Clontibret (1595)
MONAGHAN (MacMahon)

CAVAN

THE PALE
MEATH

Rathmullan
Farsetmore (1567)
R. Swilly
Lough Swilly
TYRCONNELL
Donegal

Enniskillen
Upper Lough Erne
Lough Erne
FERMANAGH
R. Arney (1594)
Belleek (1593)
Ballyshannon

BREFNI

Killybegs
Donegal Bay

LEITRIM
Sligo
SLIGO
R. Unin
Curlew (1599)
Lough Key
Boyle

0 10 20 30 Miles

renounced the 'usurped primacy and authority of the Roman Pontiff', and promised to serve the Crown with 70 horsemen, 120 kerne and as many Scots. This laid the foundation for an alliance between the Dublin administration and the O'Donnells which lasted until the 1580s [**doc. 13**]. In 1542 Con O'Neill was persuaded to visit the court at Greenwich, and there he was invested with the sword and belt of the earldom of Tyrone. In return O'Neill agreed to forsake the name of The O'Neill, to use English habits, 'and to their knowledge the English language', to practise tillage and build houses, to obey English law and to hold his lands by knight service (**16**, pp. 108–11).

THE RISE OF SHANE O'NEILL

Con O'Neill's successor under the principle of primogeniture was his son Matthew, who had been created Baron of Dungannon. This arrangement, however, clashed directly with the brehon law succession by tanistry [**doc. 1**]. Another son, Shane O'Neill, had been chosen as his father's tanist and he at once claimed that Matthew was a bastard, sprung from his father's liaison with a blacksmith's wife. Not long afterwards Matthew was waylaid and murdered, and old Con O'Neill was ousted from his ancestral lands in Tyrone and forced to seek refuge in the Pale, where he died soon after. Shane confirmed his claims under brehon law by going to the rath at Tullahogue in east Tyrone where the ceremonial inauguration of the O'Neills customarily took place. There, in Shane's own words, 'all the lords and gentlemen of Ulster assembled themselves, and . . . by one assent . . . they did elect and choose me to be O'Neill, and by that name did call me' (**6, 59**).

Here was a powerful challenge to the encroachments of the new Tudor order. Shane knew that he would have to build up his military strength rapidly in order to maintain himself. He began by bringing over some 1,500 mercenaries from Scotland. They were Campbells, McLeans, MacLeods and McKays from Kintyre and Islay, who crossed over for a season's service in Ireland. These were the 'Redshanks', so called presumably because they protected their shins with leggings of red deerskin (**75, 74**). Secondly, Shane broke with the long-standing tradition that only freemen could bear arms by arming 'all the peasants of his country, the first that ever did so of an

Irishman'. This arming of the despised 'churls' greatly augmented Shane's military strength, and gave him an enormous advantage—at least on paper—over the government, which had only about 300 cavalry, 800 infantry and 300 Irish kerne at its disposal. The kerne were essentially light infantrymen, armed with swords and spears, and with a sharp dagger (like the *skean dhu* of the Scottish highlander) stuck into their stockings. They charged with a shrill, ear-splitting yell, and were admirable auxiliaries in the hit-and-run tactics of warfare in Ireland (**74, 111**).

Shane presented a formidable challenge to the government. In May 1560 his troops were pillaging and burning on the northern borders of the Pale itself, and even causing alarm in Dundalk. The Lord Deputy, Sussex, hamstrung by lack of men and money, was forced to play for time and watch Shane's power grow still greater with the seizure of Calvach O'Donnell and his wife, the former Countess of Argyle, in spring 1561. She had admired Shane's boldness and ambition and had betrayed her husband to him. Calvach was thrown into a dungeon, loaded with chains, while Lady O'Donnell became Shane's mistress (**6, 18**). By this coup Shane gained control over most of Ulster between Lough Neagh and the Atlantic—but at the price of offending the O'Donnells.

ENGLISH ATTEMPTS TO CURB SHANE

Shane was proclaimed a rebel and a traitor and Sussex marched north, occupying Armagh, Ireland's ancient ecclesiastical capital, in July 1561. Shane withdrew, for it was not his policy to face the English forces openly in the field. Sussex was thus brought face to face with one of the prime problems of Irish warfare, that of forcing a decisive action. It was indeed true that, 'lacking the encumbrance of towns, guarded by woods and bogs and mountains, and retaining much mobility, Irish communities were hard to dominate' (**62**). This was particularly so in Ulster, the wildest province of all, where the old Gaelic patterns of life had not been modified by towns and trade or the influence of the Anglo-Irish lordships, as in Munster and Leinster (**106, 74, 61, 33**).

Sussex was baffled by the guerrilla methods of Shane's kerne, 'Never making good any fight, but bogering with his shot and flying from bush to bush ... they hold it no dishonour to run away; for the best sconce and castle for their security is their feet' (**18**). He retreated to Newry, a valuable base between Down and Armagh which had been granted to Sir Nicholas Bagenal, the Marshal of the army, during the reign of Edward VI. Here Sussex gathered a force of between six and seven hundred English troops, plus some Scottish mercenaries and some of the 'Queen's Irish kerne'. From Newry this force marched through Armagh, across the river Blackwater into Shane's territories in Tyrone, and down the Mourne-Strule valley to Lough Foyle. On this march Sussex captured some 4,000 cattle and a number of brood mares, most of which had to be killed as they could not be carried away (**74, 18**). In spite of this enormous material loss Shane still refused to give battle, and these fabian tactics forced Sussex to retrace his march back to Newry without having come to grips with Shane. Nevertheless, it was a remarkable expedition, demonstrating as it did the power to enter and devastate the O'Neill patrimony, but not to conquer it. Ulster, west of Lough Neagh now lay open to fresh penetration, a course subsequently pursued with increasing degrees of success by Sir Henry Sidney, Essex and Mountjoy.

A dramatic and largely unexpected result of this demonstration of English power was that Shane was persuaded to visit London early in 1562 [**doc. 3**]. Elizabeth issued a safe-conduct, and Shane insisted on being accompanied by the two Geraldine Earls of Kildare and Desmond, who were his kinsmen. On arrival at court Shane made a cringing and equivocal submission to the Queen in person, howling and lamenting in the Gaelic manner. He protested his right as a legitimate son to exclude Matthew of Dungannon from the succession in Tyrone. In doing so he ignored the brehon law provisions for the legitimisation of bastard sons by their fathers; however, he also implied that acceptance of primogeniture as the principle of succession was unacceptable to the O'Neills. Significantly, Shane pointed out to the Queen that Con's surrender of his title and lands to Henry VIII was of no value, since Con, as a Gaelic chieftain had only a life interest in his title and estates, and had therefore no right of alienation in brehon law. Shane concluded, with a touch of pride, that he was the true heir properly chosen by the freemen of the sept under the ancient custom of tanistry (**60, 17**, p. 72).

Elizabeth was in a quandary. She solved her problem by enlisting Shane to drive out the Scots who had settled in the Glens of Antrim, and in the district between the rivers Bann and Bush known as the

Route. These Scots were MacDonnells, Macauleys and others whose settlement in the Glens began on a large scale after the marriage of Margery Bissett, the heiress of the 'Glynnes', to James MacDonald, the Lord of the Isles, at the end of the fourteenth century. During the fifteenth century the Scots came over, mainly as gallowglasses ('foreign soldiers') willing to be employed in the endemic warfare of Ireland. The fertility of the Glens of Antrim, and their proximity to Scotland, encouraged the Scots to settle down in the north-east corner of Ireland, so adding a complicating factor to the tangled Irish situation. For Scotland, their motherland, was independent of and frequently hostile to England, and throughout Elizabeth's reign Scottish influence was an important, if fluctuating, factor in Ulster (**59, 75**).

It was government policy to try to contain this Scottish influence in Ulster, and even to attempt to root the Scots out of the province altogether. Therefore Elizabeth thought Shane's aggressiveness might well be turned to these ends, and he was dismissed from court on the understanding that he would serve the Queen against 'the robbers of the Hebrides'. This did not mean that Shane had become Elizabeth's catspaw, or that she was fool enough to trust him. In 1563 Sussex again took the field against Shane. Once more he met with nothing but frustration. His men were ambushed, a handful of Shane's Scottish gallowglasses were killed, and it was noted that Shane's men were now equipped with arquebuses. Sussex twice crossed the river Blackwater—the frontier between Armagh and Tyrone. He even reached beyond Dungannon to the ceremonial inauguration stone of the O'Neills at Tullahogue. But these forays were frustrating and indecisive, and Sussex was forced to play for time. A treaty was made with Shane in September 1563, by which he was officially recognised as 'O'Neill', but not as Earl of Tyrone (**19, 6**). It was at this stage that an attempt was made—with official connivance—to end matters by sending Shane a cask of poisoned wine for his cellars. The attempt failed, probably because Shane was an experienced drinker who habitually recovered from his potations by having himself buried up to his neck in the earth (**6, 74**).

Shane now contemptuously released Calvach O'Donnell, whom he had kept prisoner, cruelly chained, for nearly three years. Calvach was indeed a broken man. He went to Dublin, and thence to London, where Elizabeth had some 'compassion on him in this extremity, especially considering his first entry thereto was by taking part against Shane when he made war against our own good subjects there'. But neither in London nor at the Scottish court did Calvach get any real help. The O'Donnells were left to work out their own salvation (**59,** p. 130; **6,** chapter xxii).

DEFEAT OF THE MACDONNELLS

Shane O'Neill was now at the apex of his career. At this point, if he had held his hand, he might have remained in enjoyment of his office and lands long enough, like his successor Turlough Luineach O'Neill. But fate, and to some extent his promise to the Queen, drove him on to launch an attack against the MacDonnells in the late autumn of 1564, thus initiating the train of events which led to his death. The chief MacDonnells at this time were James MacDonnell and his younger brother Sorley Boy, sons of Alexander MacDonnell, Lord of Islay and Kintyre, and great-great-grandsons of John MacDonald of the Isles. Sorley Boy was in many ways a counterpart of Shane's: like Shane he was regarded with suspicion by the government, and had indeed been imprisoned in Dublin castle in 1551–2. By 1558 he and his brother James had forced the MacQuillans of the Route to acknowledge their overlordship, and so they had extended and strengthened the Scottish grip on the north-east corner (**4, 59**).

Shane therefore began his attack on the MacDonnells by attempting to take Sorley Boy's outpost at Coleraine, which controlled a strategic crossing of the lower Bann. This move was repulsed, although Sorley was wounded in the action. Shane retreated, and in the spring of 1565 collected a strong force on the northern shores of Lough Neagh. He marched thence towards the MacDonnell country in north Antrim. The MacDonnells raised the alarm, and blazing beacons on Torr Head summoned their kinsmen from Scotland. Led by Sorley's brother James, the Scottish reinforcements landed at Cushendun, only to find that Shane had attacked the castle at Red Bay and 'bracke it to the ground rather than the Skotts should again enjoy the same'. The MacDonnell brothers now joined forces at Ballycastle, where they awaited Shane's onslaught.

The opposing sides joined in battle on the morning of 2 May 1565 at Glenshesk, just a few miles south of Ballycastle. The fight that followed was bloody and furious. All day long they strove in the glen, but towards evening it was clear that the O'Neills were the victors. Thirteen MacDonnell ensigns and banners were taken, James and Sorley Boy were made prisoner, and some seven hundred Scots were killed. James MacDonnell, who had been badly wounded, was imprisoned in one of Shane's strongholds where his injuries festered and he died of neglect. Sorley Boy was dragged off with the victorious army to Dunseverick castle, which surrendered immediately, and thence to the rock fortress of Dunluce, built upon a promontory jutting out into the Atlantic. For three days the garrison held out, and for three days Sorley was kept without food. So, rather than allow Shane to starve Sorley to death in their sight, the garrison surrendered. Only by such a stratagem, or by the use of artillery, could Dunluce have been taken.

Shane had now amply fulfilled that service against the 'robbers of the Hebrides' which he had promised the Queen in 1562. He had also asserted the supremacy of his name over a greater portion of Ulster than had even been accomplished previously, but, in doing so he had made deadly enemies of the MacDonnells, a fact observed with a quiet satisfaction by the government (**59, 6, 18**).

SIR HENRY SIDNEY'S EXPEDITION, 1566

The Lord Deputyship had now passed from Sussex, who had been in office since 1556, to his young kinsman Sir Henry Sidney. Sidney proved to be one of the ablest of Elizabeth's viceroys in Ireland, although, unlike his predecessor, he was not given the more honorific title of Lord Lieutenant. Further, to save expense he was allowed to continue in office as Lord President of Wales. This financial cheese-paring was also reflected in the inadequate military forces at his disposal. The nucleus of Sidney's army comprised about 880 infantry and 300 Irish kerne—the sepoys of the Irish campaigns (**74, 98**). In addition, there was the clumsy medieval expedient of the 'hosting of the Englishry' in the Pale, which produced a nominal force of 3000 plus some 500 gallowglasses. As for Shane, Sidney reported that 'Lucifer was never more puffed up with pride and ambition than O'Neill is. He continually keepeth six hundred armed men about him and is able to bring into the field one thousand horsemen and four thousand foot. He is the only strong man of Ireland, his country was never so rich or inhabited, and he armest

and weaponeth all the peasants of his country . . .' (**6,** chapter xxiv).
Yet against such odds Sidney was prepared to take the field.

The object of Sidney's expedition was to weaken Shane by
establishing a post on Lough Foyle, and restoring the O'Donnells in
Tyrconnell and the Maguires in Fermanagh. On 17 September 1566,
somewhat late in the campaigning season, Sidney and his young
lieutenant Humphrey Gilbert began their march from Drogheda.
Simultaneously, Colonel Randolph's small force landed on the
western shore of Lough Foyle and built a fort at Derry. Sidney
found Armagh in ruins, so he marched onwards to the mouth of the
river Blackwater and captured Coney Island in Lough Neagh.
On this island was one of Shane O'Neill's strongholds called
'Fuath-na-gall', meaning 'Detestation of the foreigners'. Here was a
stone tower thirty feet high, surrounded by a thick hedge and
'bearded with stakes and other sharp wood', defended by a ditch
ten feet wide and four feet deep, with a stone-faced rampart along
its inner edge. This was Shane's treasury, where he stored his plate,
jewels and apparel. To commemorate this exploit Sidney decided
to call Lough Neagh and Coney Island after himself, and placed
James Vaughan in command of a small garrison on the island
(**17, 92**).

Crossing the Blackwater with the main body of his troops, Sidney
marched to the ancient ecclesiastical centre of Clogher, and thence
northwards down the Mourne-Strule valley to rendezvous with
Randolph at Lifford, fourteen miles upstream from the fort at Derry.
Having thus successfully repeated Sussex's traverse of Shane's lands
in 1561, Sidney marched his force back to the Pale through Donegal,
Sligo and Athlone (**74**). This whole expedition was an impressive
method of 'showing the flag', and it succeeded in curbing Shane's
overweening ambition by the restoration of the O'Donnells. Further
Shane's inability or unwillingness to face government forces in the
field had again been demonstrated, and both his pride and his
pocket had been hurt by the capture of Coney Island. These factors
pointed ominously not only to the downfall of Shane, but to the
ultimate ending of the power of the princely O'Neills in the north.
Randolph's hold on Derry, however, was tenuous. His force was
attacked by Shane's troops, and he himself was killed. The powder
magazine in the fort at Derry accidentally blew up in April 1567
and the demoralised garrison withdrew by sea to Carrickfergus.
Nonetheless, Shane's position had been undermined. He had lost

many of his Scottish mercenaries, his lands had been penetrated by invasion and rapine, his enemies had been restored. To redress the balance he decided to attack the O'Donnells.

FARSETMORE AND CUSHENDUN

> Ring the alarum-bell! Blow, wind! come, wrack!
> At least we'll die with harness on our back!
>
> W. SHAKESPEARE, *Macbeth*, V, v.

In May 1567 Shane collected together his forces and marched to the southern shore of the river Swilly, just below Letterkenny. On the other side of the river Hugh O'Donnell lay ensconced behind earthen ramparts. Shane impetuously advanced to the attack, fording the river estuary at low water. He was opposed by O'Donnell's lightly armed horsemen, who advanced into battle shouting their war cry, brandishing their lances overarm in the Irish fashion, and riding their garrons (hacks) without saddle or stirrup (**111**). The ensuing battle of Farsetmore lasted for several hours. The *Four Masters* wrote as if describing an Homeric conflict of the gods:

Fierce and desperate were the grim and terrible looks that each cast at the other out of their starlike eyes; they raised the battle-cry aloud, and their united shouting, when rushing together, was sufficient to strike with dismay and turn to flight the feeble and unwarlike. They proceeded to strike, mangle, slaughter, and cut down one another for a long time, so that men were soon laid low, heroes wounded, youths slain, and robust heroes mangled in the slaughter (**29**).

The battle of Farsetmore was not, as the annalists appear to have thought, just another episode in the dreary tale of internecine fighting amongst the Gaelic or Anglo-Irish lords. It was in fact one of the decisive events heralding the ending of the old order (**79**). Shane was worsted and forced to retreat across the Swilly, now swollen by the full tide. Many of his men were drowned in the crossing, though Shane himself escaped with a small band by fording the river further upstream. According to the *Four Masters* Shane lost in this battle 1,300 men; according to Sir Henry Sidney—the *tertius gaudens* of this conflict—613 men (**74**).

The last act of the drama was now at hand. Like Macbeth, Shane now appeared to have lost all sense of proportion or common prudence. In his extremity he wrote to the MacDonnells for help. Alexander MacDonnell crossed over from Kintyre with a great fleet, and encamped at Cushendun in the Glens of Antrim. Shortly afterwards Shane rode in with his tattered bodyguard of fifty men, bringing with them Sorley Boy, who had been kept a prisoner since the defeat of the MacDonnells at Glenshesk in 1565. After a day or two a feast was prepared, Shane became inebriated, and a quarrel flared up:

> Out sprang Aspucke, and beat O'Neills man, and then suddenly brought his band upon them in the tent, where the soldiers, with their slaughter-knives, killed the secretary and Shane O'Neill, mangling him cruelly, lapped him in an old Irish shirt, and tumbled him into a pit, within an old Chappell hard by: whose head four days after Captain Piers [the constable of Carrickfergus castle] cut off and met therewith the [Lord] Deputy, who sent it before him staked on a pole to the castle of Dublin (**59,** pp. 140–4).

Shane's death relieved the administration of a 'false, perjured, seditious and pernicious conspirer, rebel, and traitor'. The Queen was pleased by the news, and wrote to Sidney on 5 July 1567 that, 'We have thought it not impertinent to let you know how well we think of you for this service done in Ulster' (**6, 18**). Two years later by an act of attainder the sovereignty of the O'Neills was abolished. This was a legalistic method of attacking the basis of power of any Gaelic chief, and it was a clear assertion of the government's determination that English law and customs would prevail over the Gaelic order. Indeed, the abolition of the sovereignty of the O'Neills meant a reassertion of the Queen's authority as the lawful successor to the medieval earldom of Ulster [**doc. 9**]. Finally Shane's death cleared the way for the first Elizabethan experiments in colonisation in Ireland.

4 The Enterprise of Ulster

For that is the evil which now I find in all Ireland, that the Irish
dwell together by their septs and several nations, so as they may
practise or conspire what they will; whereas if there were English
well placed among them, they should not be able once to stir or to
murmur . . .

EDMUND SPENSER, *A View of the State of Ireland*, in (**21**), p. 165

The death of Shane O'Neill presented the government with an
opportunity to intervene more fully in Ulster. Yet, with typical
Elizabethan financial stringency, this many-faceted problem was
not tackled, as Mary had attempted to do in the case of Leix and
Offaly, but was left to the enterprise of private speculators and
adventurers. Small wonder that the outcome of this 'enterprise of
Ulster' was not successful, although in the field of colonial theory it
proved immensely fruitful not only in the plantation of Ulster but in
the colonisation of Virginia and Massachusetts (**9, 63, 115**).

The first in the field was the young Humphrey Gilbert, who had
served under Randolph at Derry, and who had been chosen by Sir
Henry Sidney to carry a dispatch on the failure of that expedition to
London. Gilbert was full of ideas of colonisation, and saw that there
was a splendid opportunity for young adventurers like himself to
form a company for establishing a plantation, bringing over artisans
and founding settlements which might develop into towns. Indeed
it was proposed that Gilbert might be made the 'President' of Ulster
in return for organising and establishing the plantation. This
indicated the official realisation that Ulster, and later Munster and
Connacht, required a more effective form of provincial administration comparable to that provided by the Council of Wales or the
Council of the North [**doc. 26**].

SIR THOMAS SMITH AND THE ARDS COLONY

Gilbert's Ulster schemes came to nothing and he switched his
attention to the more promising province of Munster (see chapter 5).
Four years later a fresh scheme for the colonisation of part of Ulster
was propounded by Sir Thomas Smith. Smith was born on 28 March

1512 at Saffron Walden, Essex, the son of John Smith, a prosperous sheep farmer. Beginning as a 'Poor scholar', Smith had a brilliant academic career. He was elected a Fellow of Queen's College, Cambridge, in 1531, and became Public Orator of the University. A lively Renaissance scholar, Smith attempted to introduce a new pronunciation of Greek, and invented a reformed alphabet of twenty-nine letters for English (**64, 65**). Such a brilliant man was soon induced to serve in politics. He was employed by Somerset in 1547, and was made Secretary of State and knighted in 1548. Other offices fell to him. He became Steward of the Stannaries (**69**), Dean of Carlisle cathedral and Provost of Eton. But, if the rewards were glittering, the risks were proportionate, for on Somerset's fall Smith was sent to the Tower. Released later, he lived quietly until the sunshine days of Elizabeth (**64**). As a member of the Privy Council in 1571 he was concerned with Irish matters, and took the opportunity to initiate the 'most honourable and princely enterprise that Her Majesty ought to take in hand', namely the plantation of the Ards peninsula in eastern Ulster as a preliminary step towards the reduction of Down and Antrim, and, secondly, of the unsubdued lands west of the river Bann and Lough Neagh.

Sir Thomas Smith's interest in colonisation had its roots in his classical readings and had been stimulated by accounts of the voyages of discovery and the colonial experiments already carried out in the New World. 'To Smith, the English in Ireland were the modern Romans, bringing to a savage land law, peace, and civilization' (**115**). The colony to be established in the Ards peninsula was to emulate a Roman colony by being organised initially on a military basis: 'I and my deputies be in dede *Coloniae ductores*, the distributors of land to english men in a forein contrey, and as they who so take land be *Coloni*, or Coloners, so we that do distribute it may be called . . . Colonells.' The area selected for the colony—the Ards peninsula—could be easily defended by small garrisons placed on the 'strait neck of land, by which it was joyned to the rest of the island'. The colonists were to be defended by foot-soldiers and cavalry, who would be sustained by the produce of specified proportions of land. For the first seven years the colony was to be regarded as a military frontier, and within this framework the native Irish were to be contained and pacified, 'that those half barbarous people might be taught some civility'. This indicated that Sir Thomas was indeed an 'armchair empire builder', for most of the inhabitants

of the Ards were descended from Norman settlers introduced by
John de Courcy, who could scarcely be dismissed as 'mere' Irish
(**115**).

Smith's proposal was accepted by the government in November
1571 and letters patent granted to him and his illegitimate son
Thomas (b. 1547) the lands of the 'Ardes in Clandeboye, which lieth
south to the castle called Belfast, so to the abbey or priory called
Massereene, the castle called Castle Mowbray and the Castle
Toome', to hold from the crown as tenants of the earldom of Ulster.
Sir Thomas was now posted to France as ambassador, and the
execution of the enterprise was left to his son Thomas, whom the
father regarded as a 'fantastical fool'. Seven to eight hundred men
were collected together and this motley band hung about Liverpool
during the sharp winter of 1571–2. By the spring the numbers had
diminished, and through mismanagement and official delays, it was
not until the end of August that a mere one hundred landed on the
shores of Strangford Lough, 'not enough to set out the main chance'.
They were actively opposed by Sir Brian McPhelim O'Neill, the
lord of Clandeboy, who had been greatly angered by the grant of so
much of his ancestral territory to the Smiths. A colony made at the
expense of existing landlords and clearly designed to rest on a base
of Irish servile labour was bound to meet with determined opposition. The Ards was invaded by a force of O'Neill's men who burnt the
ancient abbeys of Newtown, Movilla, Bangor and Holywood, lest
they should provide shelter for the invaders. Young Smith and his
crew were forced to retreat for a time to the shelter of Carrickfergus
castle, although they did succeed in establishing a post at Comber,
where they survived the winter of 1572–3. But in August Smith
was killed by the 'revolting of certain Irishmen of his own household,
to whom he overmuch trusteth, whereof one being retained by a rebel
did kill him with a shot' (**46, 109, 115, 6**).

For a time Sir Thomas Smith collapsed. Both his son and his
attempted plantation of the Ards had gone. But in December 1574
he roused himself for a fresh effort. This time he proposed that the
settlers should live in small towns. The focus of the colony was to be
a walled city, 'which I would were called *Elizabetha*. . . . Choose a
place strong by nature for defence as a citidel, to defend the city
when it shall be made, and then it may be called *Castra colonelli* or
Smith's tents, for so long till it have a better name' (**115**). Smith's
plan was full of convincing detail on paper (**64,** pp. 164–8). It was

another matter to put it into practice. There were many delays, so much so that in March 1574 the Queen herself ordered Smith to 'send some force into the Ardes to strengthen such as shall inhabit in Clandeboy, or else shall be compounded withal for his interest'. Sir Thomas was too old to go across in person, so he appointed his brother George and captain Jerome Brett to set out with a token force of 150 men. Needless to say such a body could make no headway against the fury of the Clandeboy O'Neills, and there could be no question of colonising the Ards peninsula. Reluctantly, Smith was forced to hand over his cherished enterprise to the Earl of Essex. He died in August 1577, the pioneer of colonising ideas which bore fruit a generation later (**115, 108, 64, 65**).

ESSEX IN ANTRIM

The future progress of colonisation in Ulster now hinged on Walter Devereux, the first Earl of Essex. Like Smith, a private adventurer, Essex had produced a plan for the settlement of Antrim in 1573. This plan had received support from such highly placed figures as Burghley, Sussex and Leicester (**71**). The Queen herself lent Essex £10,000 on a mortgage of his English property, and he was granted the lands from Knockfergus Bay (Belfast Lough) to Lough Sidney and the lower Bann, excepting Carrickfergus castle, which remained the property of the Crown. Essex was also granted the Glens of Antrim, the Route and the island of Rathlin. Altogether, this meant the greater part of Antrim, with the 'liberty of several fishings of the Bann and Lough Neagh adjoining to the said countries, and liberty of free fishing in all the Lough'. Essex also had authority to 'annoy by fire and sword ... any of the Irishry or Scottish Irish that is a notorious offender or malefactor'. He was further authorised to 'spoil, beseige, raze, or burn any castle, house, fort, or fortress of any outlaws, rebels or felons'. Finally, he was enabled to 'alien to men of English birth all the lands of the said country ... except the land belonging to the town of Knockfergus' (**17**, pp. 257–8). In all these transactions the prescriptive rights and interests of the O'Neills of Clandeboy, the MacDonnells of the Glens and the MacQuillans of the Route were brushed aside—an attitude which typified the lack of understanding between the Elizabethan adventurers and the Anglo-Irish and Gaelic landowners, which bedevilled affairs in

37

Munster, and which also affected the relationship between colonists and aboriginal population in both north and south America. In face of such 'conquistadors' as Essex what choice had the older land-owners but recourse to the sword to defend their properties (**10, 34, 63**)?

To establish his claim to his newly granted lands, Essex collected together six pieces of artillery, large quantities of gunpowder and slow matches, trenching tools, 150 calivers (light muskets), 60 muskets, together with 200 bowmen, and two surgeons at a salary of 16 shillings a month. Other adventurers joined his standard, for instance Lord Rich with 100 men, who hoped to establish himself at Red Bay castle in the Glens of Antrim. Rich, however, became 'heartily sick' of the expedition, and returning to England married Essex's daughter Penelope Devereux. The marriage ended in divorce, and the lady subsequently married Charles Blount, Lord Mountjoy, the eventual conqueror of Ulster. Sir Arthur Champer-nowne collected together forty men, and looked to his territorial reward at Dunseverick. William and John Norris proposed to settle near Ballycastle, while Sir Peter Carew indulged his appetite for land speculations in Ireland by supplying a further forty men to support the enterprise (**59**, pp. 416–21). Small wonder that Essex felt confident of success. The Queen, always politic in such matters, advised him to have consideration of the Irish, who had become disobedient subjects largely through the influence of the Scots. To her Essex replied, in terms which would have fitted Cromwell, that he 'would not willingly imbrue his hands with more blood than the necessity of the cause requireth' (**19**).

Essex sailed from Liverpool on 16 August 1573. The expedition landed on the Copeland islands, and realising their error, made their way thence to the shelter of Carrickfergus. Essex had not been there long before he began to see the disadvantages of waging war as a private contractor. It was clear that nothing would answer in such a case but success. Accordingly, Essex advanced to the lower Bann, which formed the boundary between his land grant and the lands of the O'Neills and the O'Cahans. Shane O'Neill's successor, Turlough Luineach O'Neill, a lethargic but prudent man, was summoned to assist Essex against the Scots of Antrim, whose lands had been assigned on paper to the gentlemen adventurers in Essex's force, and who were doubtless anxious to secure some return on their investment. Turlough O'Neill was curtly informed that his assistance might find him grace with her Majesty; the alternative was to have his properties laid waste. Turlough's kinsman, Sir Brian McPhelim O'Neill, also received peremptory instructions to submit in the Queen's name to Essex. To underline these orders herds of cattle were impounded in the vicinity of Carrickfergus. Essex fondly thought these animal hostages to be secure, but they were duly recovered by the united efforts of the Tyrone and Clandeboy O'Neills, who showed Essex what experienced cattle raiders could accomplish. Essex now began to be disillusioned and embittered. He blamed the poor support he had got from the gentlemen adventurers, who lacked 'resolute minds to endure the travail of a year or two in this waste country', and he grumbled about the common soldiers 'who grow to mutiny . . .; so as my humble desire is that some mean may be devised how her Majesty may more effectually countenance this war. . . . And for a present needful supply I desire 200 footmen to be embarked at Chester and Liverpool, with all convenient speed' (**6, 59,** p. 421).

Meanwhile, the Queen had written to Mr Secretary Burghley expressing her dislike of the 'enterprise of Ulster, for default of them who should execute it'. She asked, 'what men of Council or Wisdom there were, into whose hand might be committed so great a Mass of Money, and so great a charge as should be sent'. In short, should Essex not be removed and placated by being appointed as Lord Deputy of Ireland? In the event, by a typical compromise, he was appointed Governor of Ulster—and starved of adequate supplies of men and money. Essex, indeed, was now so deeply involved in his Irish colonial venture that he was prepared to mortgage the rest of his English property. But such a resolve did not feed or clothe his men. Not even the arrival of reinforcements offset the wastage through sickness and desertion of between fifteen and twenty men each day. Nevertheless Essex doggedly persisted in his efforts to subdue Sir Brian O'Neill, his most immediate opponent. A price of £200 was placed on Sir Brian's head, and surprisingly enough he submitted.

THE ATTACK ON THE O'NEILLS

Early in 1574 Essex attacked a crannog (a fortified lake dwelling) near Banbridge, whence the O'Neills had been raiding the Magennis lands of Iveagh in Down. He followed up this successful foray by summoning Turlough Luineach O'Neill to meet him at Benburb on the river Blackwater. Naturally enough Turlough refused and Essex promptly crossed the river, laying waste all that he could from Benburb to Clogher, and even penetrating as far as the wild and boggy Maguire lands in Fermanagh. He then turned north, marching down the Mourne-Strule valley in the footsteps of Sussex and Sidney and parleying with O'Donnell at Lifford. However, as in previous incursions west of the Bann, the trail of damage was soon repaired, for there were no towns and few stone houses. Essex quickly saw the point that only permanent forts in the wilderness, garrisoned by the Queen's troops, could bring any permanent military advantage by subjugating western Ulster. The Queen approved this plan for settling Ulster, but refused to allow Essex adequate support in carrying out his schemes. Ironically, the building of forts proved to be the beginning of the end for the O'Neill power a generation later. Essex complained to Burghley that his plans could not be properly implemented, 'either because of Her Majesty's misliking of the cause, or of me as unable to execute the thing, and so make stay of me there, either by disallowing the work as not feasible, or else to essay as the honour of it should be reaped by another'. In such shabby treatment Essex was not alone.

Meanwhile, Essex vented his bitterness and frustration upon Sir Brian McPhelim O'Neill: 'I have apprehended Sir Brian, his half-brother Rory Oge MacQuillan, Brian's wife, and certain of the principal persons, and put others to the sword, to the number of 200 in all places, whereof forty were his best horsemen.' This noteworthy event took place in Belfast, then a handful of cottages clustered near the church and small castle at the ford of the river Lagan, a place regarded by Essex as 'meet for a corporate town, armed with all commodities, as a principal haven, wood and good ground' (**46**). Here, according to the *Annals of the Four Masters*:

> They passed three nights and days together pleasantly and cheerfully. At the expiration of this time, as they were agreeably eating and making merry, Brian, his brother, and his wife, were seized upon by the Earl, and all his people put unsparingly to the sword . . . in Brian's own presence. Brian was afterwards sent in chains to Dublin, together with his wife and brother, where they were cut in quarters. Such was the end of their feast (**29**).

No blame for this ruthless atrocity—the Irish analogue of the

40

notorious 'Feast of Black Douglas' in Edinburgh castle—was ever issued. As for Essex his only comment was that 'This little execution hath broke the faction and made them all afeard' (**6, 19, 46**).

Essex now returned to the larger project of subduing the O'Neill lands west of Lough Neagh and the river Blackwater. Ever hopeful, he estimated that a body of 1,300 men in garrisons would suffice to hold these lands once they were conquered. Clearly Turlough must be brought to heel for 'without the rooting out and abating of Turlough's strength neither the English Pale can live in quiet nor Ulster be reduced to any conformity'. Essex was instructed by letter from the Privy Council to deal with Turlough 'either by force or capitulation . . . [or] extirpation by force, as the surest and soundest way of redress'. Thus encouraged in his plan Essex began to cut 'passes' through woods bordering Tyrone, so that the way could be opened for an attack. But once more Elizabeth retreated and refused to guarantee the necessary support. Essex forthwith resigned his governorship of Ulster. In effect, this provided Turlough O'Neill with a tactical victory, for he announced that he was only prepared to parley with an official representative of the Crown (**19**).

THE RATHLIN MASSACRE

The disgruntled Essex withdrew to Drogheda where he received a missive from the Queen which stated clearly that the attempt to reduce Ulster must either pay its way or be abandoned. This spurred him to return to the Blackwater frontier, where he began to construct a bridge over the river protected by an entrenched enclosure. This work was never completed, for, as might have been expected, it was perpetually harassed by Turlough O'Neill's men and by his ally Sorley Boy MacDonnell. Essex managed to repulse Turlough, then turned to attack Sorley Boy. He drove him out of Clandeboy, and followed this up with an attack on the storm-girt island of Rathlin off the north Antrim coast. The expedition sailed from Carrickfergus in July 1575 under John Norris, one of the gentlemen adventurers under Essex, and with Francis Drake, already established as a sea-dog, in command of the *Falcon*. They coasted north and, having landed on Rathlin, stormed Robert the Bruce's old castle, killing some 200 of its defenders. No quarter was given and between 300 and 400 other people were hunted down in their refuges along the cliffs and in souterrains and mercilessly slain. 'Sorley Boy and his gentlemen sent their wives and children to Rathlin, who are all executed. Sorley stood on the mainland and saw the taking of the island, which made him run mad', Essex wrote exultantly to Walsingham. In the storming of Rathlin eleven of the MacDonnell galleys were destroyed, and a total of 300 cattle, 3,000 sheep, 300 brood mares and provisions for 300 men for twelve months, fell to the victors. Rathlin, however, though easy to sack, was difficult to hold. Norris and Drake were forced to abandon it, largely under the pressure of Sorley Boy's counterattack against the garrison of Carrickfergus. Nevertheless, the MacDonnells were sore wounded by this massacre on their offshore base, and Sorley Boy fled into exile in Scotland, where he remained for the next decade (**59**, pp. 183–6).

Essex now withdrew to Waterford, and in October 1575 landed in Pembrokeshire where he still possessed some property. Elizabeth consoled him by telling him that, 'neither your mind's care, your body's toil, nor purse's charge was unprofitably employed' (**18**). He was granted the barony of Farney in co. Monaghan, and was installed for life in the office of Earl Marshal. He returned to Ireland, arriving in Dublin on 23 July 1576, but by September was racked by sickness and depression. He grew worse, was attacked by dysentery, took to his bed and died. His rival Leicester married his widow (**71, 107**). It was an ironic end to a career filled with a fatal infatuation for Ireland, an infatuation that was eventually to lead his son to the block.

5 The Desmond Rebellion in Munster

> How could communities,
> ...
> The primogenitive and due of birth,
> Prerogative of age, crown, sceptres, laurels,
> But by degree, stand in authentic place?
> Take but degree away, untune that string,
> And, hark, what discord follows! Each thing meets
> In mere oppugnancy ...
> Force should be right; or, rather, right and wrong, —
> Between whose endless jar justice resides, —
> Should lose their names, and so should justice too.
>
> W. SHAKESPEARE, *Troilus and Cressida*, I; iii.

The violent career of Shane O'Neill had clearly indicated to the governments in Dublin and London that the reduction of Gaelic Ireland to English law was going to be a task of considerable magnitude. Sussex, Sidney and Essex had also learnt the elements of the military problems confronting them, and the latter had realised that garrisons financed and sustained by the government could curb the unsubdued areas, and might prepare the way for a successful policy of plantation. Colonisation, indeed, was much in men's minds and its underlying theories made clearer by the writings with which Sir Thomas Smith preceded his disastrous practical attempts to make a settlement in the Ards. Ulster, however, with its lack of towns and poor communications, was the most difficult area in which to begin the process of 'reducing Ireland to civility' as Humphrey Gilbert had already found. The richer and more accessible province of Munster proved to be a more attractive magnet to the land-hungry younger sons who were beginning to swarm out of the West of England. It lay in the golden pathway which led to the treasure galleons of the Spanish Main and the Azores, and to rich and profitable plantations in the New World. Here, and not in Ulster, did the Elizabethan adventurers look for the fulfilment of Sir Thomas Smith's get-rich-quick call, 'How say you now? Have I not set forth to you another Utopia?' (**64**).

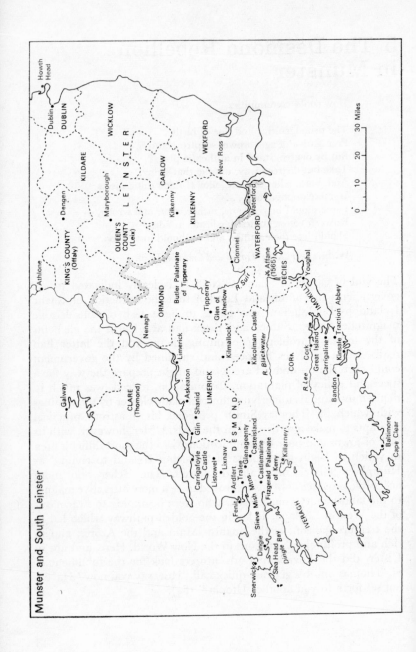

Munster and South Leinster

THE BUTLERS OF ORMOND *v* THE GERALDINES OF DESMOND

Just as the death of Shane O'Neill provided an opening for the colonising schemes of Smith and Essex, so the long-standing feud between the Butlers and the Geraldines provided an opportunity which the thrustful West Country adventurers were unlikely to miss (**62, 69, 10**). James Fitzgerald, 15th Earl of Desmond, died in 1558, and was succeeded by his second son Gerald as 16th Earl. Gerald carried on the family tradition by bickering with his stepson 'Black Tom' (Thomas Butler, 10th Earl of Ormond), over possession of three manors in south Tipperary. An armed confrontation between followers of the rival earls took place in 1560 at Corroge near Tipperary town, but 'concord was established between the hosts, for having reflected concerning the battle they parted without coming to any engagement on that occasion'. Both earls were heavily fined and bound over to keep the peace, but, in spite of this, raids and skirmishes marked the next four years. Desmond, who with his cousin the Earl of Kildare had accompanied Shane O'Neill to London in 1562, promised in addition to pay the Queen her feudal dues, and to suppress brehon law (**6,** ch. xix).

On his return to Munster, Desmond shrugged off his promises, and tried to restore his finances by attempting to squeeze tribute from the district of Decies in west Waterford. He also wished to assert the supremacy of his house over Sir Maurice Fitzgerald of the Decies, who had transferred his loyalties to the Butlers of Ormond. The business came to a head at Affane on the river Blackwater in co. Waterford on 1 February 1565. A brief battle was fought. Desmond's horsemen charged, but were repulsed with heavy loss. The Earl of Desmond was wounded and carried off a prisoner to Clonmel (**93**). Elizabeth was furious at this faction fight, of a kind already a hundred years out of date in England. She ordered both earls to cross to London, for she believed that, 'the enmity between the two earls was greater and deeplier rooted than could be reformed by any but her own princely directions'. Both earls submitted to the Crown, and entered into recognisances of £20,000 each for their future good behaviour. Ormond remained at court for the next three and a half years on the best of terms with the Queen, who encouraged Lord Deputy Sidney to favour the Ormond claims, while Desmond was kept under virtual 'house arrest' in London until 1573 (**6, 18**).

THE WEST COUNTRY ADVENTURERS

The disorder of these overmighty subjects gave various West Country adventurers their opportunity to intervene and feather their own nests in so doing. Foremost among them was Sir Peter Carew, who came from Mohun Ottery in Devon and claimed to be a descendant of Robert Fitzstephen, one of the Normans of the twelfth century who had secured lands in Leinster. The courts upheld Carew's antiquarian claims to a manor in co. Meath, and also the barony of Idrone in co. Carlow (**3, 4**). Others quickly followed suit and soon none of the older landowners could feel their titles secure against the intrusive newcomers. Sir Warham St Leger and Richard Grenville, for example, established themselves between Cork and Kinsale. They were joined by five others—Edward Saintloo, Thomas Leton, Jacques Wingfield, Gilbert Talbot and Humphrey Gilbert—and this group proposed that they should form a company for the exploitation of the rich fisheries of the Munster coasts (**67**), [**doc. 27**]. In Humphrey Gilbert's opinion this was but part of the larger enterprise of making Ireland 'civil and under subjection of good laws'. This was a desirable undertaking, for as things stood 'Ireland was more chardgeable in kepinge thereof than proffitable to England'. If Ireland were allowed to remain 'uncyvill' it would continue to be divided by faction and rebellion, open to the attacks of enemies, 'the contry apt to have ayde of Spanyardes or scottes or bothe'. The Spanish, French and Scots might well envy Ireland's fruitful soil, her castles and towns and her commodious harbours. To wrest such a kingdom from England would do her irreparable harm. Therefore, argued Gilbert, Ireland must be made 'cyvill and under subjection of good lawes'. Not only would England be secured from flank attack, but there would be a positive profit from the exploitation of lands, mines, fisheries and the expansion of trade. Gilbert suggested closing Irish trade to foreigners, establishing fortresses and garrisons, and to encourage the new English rather than the Gaelic or Anglo-Irish landowners. In particular, he propounded acceptance of his schemes for the plantation of Munster (**67**, pp. 124–8). Here were some of the ideas which flowered in 1576 into Gilbert's discourse about the North-West Passage to Cathay, and which culminated in his last voyage in 1584. But Munster was not like Baffin Land, nor were the existing landowners to be lightly brushed aside.

REBELLION OF THE ESTABLISHED LANDOWNERS

In 1569 Sir Edmund Butler, a cadet of the house of Ormond, flew into rebellion, not against the Queen, but against those 'who banish Ireland and mean conquest'. He was joined by Sir James Fitzmaurice Fitzgerald, cousin of the absent Earl of Desmond, who had been chosen in the Gaelic manner by the leading Geraldines as their 'Captain'. Fitzmaurice was an ardent supporter of the Counter-Reformation, and therefore introduced a new element into the tangle of Irish dissension, an element which was notably missing from Shane O'Neill's career in Ulster. After 1570, when the Queen was condemned as a heretic by the Bull 'Regnans in Excelsis', Fitzmaurice, and those who shared his convictions, were inevitably forced into active treason. Further, this religious involvement meant that Irish affairs assumed an increasing significance as part of the pattern of European power-politics (**1, 85, 52**).

Sir Edmund Butler and Sir James Fitzmaurice were both of Anglo-Irish or 'Old English' stock. They were joined in their rebellion by MacCarthy More, recently created Earl of Clancarthy, who represented the most important Gaelic family in Munster. He, too, had been driven into rebellion by Sir Peter Carew's land claims and Humphrey Gilbert's colonising schemes. Indeed the collaboration of Anglo-Irish and Gaelic in a common cause was perhaps the most significant result of the Elizabethan intrusion into Munster, and was destined to play an important part in the course of Irish history during the seventeenth century (**3, 2, 12**).

The rebellion began with Fitzmaurice's attack on Carrigaline castle and Tracton abbey in co. Cork, where St Leger and Sir Richard Grenville had settled. Fitzmaurice was aided in the attack on Tracton by MacCarthy More, and two of his Desmond kinsmen: the White Knight of Kilmallock and the Seneschal of Imokilly. By June 1569 the mayors of Cork and Kinsale were so alarmed that they wrote to Sidney, the Lord Deputy, 'The rebels brag that they will take Kinsale and Cork, that help cometh from Spain, and that the Butlers are of the confederacy'. They added that the land between their two towns had been devastated. The mayor of Waterford made the significant comment that, 'the good subjects in the country forced by the rebels to become partners of their confederacy, or else to end their wretched lives by famine' (**17**, pp. 167–8).

Meantime the junior branches of the Butler family had risen in rebellion in west Tipperary and in part of eastern Queen's county. Fitzmaurice cooperated with them by shifting his attack to Kilmallock in co. Limerick, a walled town capable of harbouring English troops sent from Limerick or Cork, and whose possession was of considerable strategic importance as the gateway to the heart of the Desmond lands. Simultaneously, Kilkenny was attacked in an effort to capture the very citadel of the pro-English senior Butlers, but in vain. Sir Henry Sidney sent Humphrey Gilbert to help Carew, and together they took Cloghgrenan castle from Sir Edmund Butler. This effectively ended the Butler part of the rebellion. Sir Edmund was eventually pardoned though 'he was never restored in blood and so did not inherit the Earldom in due time' (**3**, p. 191; **6**, ch. xxvi).

Sidney now relieved Cork, and in early September 1570 Humphrey Gilbert was selected as colonel of the army of Munster. This was his first independent command, earned partly by his reputation for courage ('surely there is not a vallyanter man that lyveth'), and partly by his reputation for ruthlessness. A typical Elizabethan soldier in Ireland, Gilbert devastated the countryside, spared nobody in any captured castles, and forced those who came to his tent to surrender to walk between two lines of heads severed from his enemies. He thought scornfully of the liberties written into the town charters, for 'the Prince had a Regular and absolute power, and that which might not be done by the one, I wolde do it by the other in Casez of necessatie' (**67**). He would not parley with any rebels, because he did not want them to think that 'the Queen had more need of their service, than they had of her mercy. He put many to the sword, and spared not any malefactor unexecuted that came to his hands.' All this because he believed that no conquered nation would ever yield willingly obedience for love but rather for fear. Here indeed was the true spirit of the conquistador!

By the close of 1569 the Munster rebels had been crushed, and Gilbert had acquired an almost legendary reputation for ruthlessness. Sir Walter Raleigh wrote a decade later that he had never read of any man more feared than Humphrey Gilbert among the Irish nation. In January 1570 Gilbert was knighted by the Lord Deputy at Drogheda for his Irish services, and shortly thereafter left Ireland (**18, 67**).

THE PRESIDENCY OF MUNSTER

In 1570 it was felt that the time was ripe to extend government influence by establishing presidencies in the provinces of Munster and Connacht. These presidencies were to be a form of local administration similar to those already established to deal with the special problems presented by the north of England and Wales. The president received an annual stipend of £133 6s 8d, and was advised by a council. This council was endowed with the same judicial authority as an ordinary court of assize, and was obliged to send monthly reports of its activities to the Lord Deputy and Privy Council in Dublin castle. Although the council in Munster had power to hear and determine cases, yet it was established in order to support the operation of the ordinary courts, and not to supplant them. In short, appeal lay to the council 'where any special complaint shall be made unto them of any manifest wrong or delay of justice' (**16,** pp. 111–12), rather like the functions of a modern ombudsman. The president also was to be supplied with 'some competent number of soldiers, whereby his decrees and orders justly taken and made, the more effectually may be executed'. Inevitably, in the conditions of Munster in 1570 the sword weighed heavily in the scales of justice [**doc. 11**].

The person appointed as the first Lord President of Munster was Sir John Perrot. Perrot was remarkable even in a period of illustrious men. He was supposed to be one of Henry VIII's illegitimate children, and, indeed, he certainly shared that monarch's imperious temperament: 'His countenance full of Majestie, his Eye marvellous piercing, and carrying a commanding aspect', noted for his physical strength and magnanimity of mind, yet he proved his own worst enemy for 'he was by nature very choloricke, and could not brooke any Crosses, or dissemble the least Injuries . . . whereby he procured to himselfe many and mighty Adversarys' (**26**).

Perrot began his rule in Munster by attacking James Fitzmaurice's men, who had sacked Kilmallock in March 1571. Perrot lodged in the ruined town, and encouraged the townspeople to 'buyld their Gates, to repayre the Towne-Walles, and to re-edifie their Howses'. He also vigorously pursued the rebels: 'The Lord President caused his Men to light from their Horses, to rip off their boots, and to leppe into the Bogges, taking with them their petronels and lighthorsemen's staves instead of pikes, with which they charged the enemy in the Bogges, overthrew them, and cut off fifty of their heads, which they carried home with them unto Kilmallock, and put the heads round about the (Market) Cross' (**26,** p. 52). Meantime James Fitzmaurice —'a silly wood-kerne'—roamed at will from his base in the wooded Glen of Aherlow in Tipperary as far afield as Castlemaine and Killarney in Kerry (where the palatine jurisdiction of the Desmonds had been suppressed in 1570) and the fishing ports of the southern coasts. Perrot attempted to capture Castlemaine, a stronghold which controlled the route from the Iveragh peninsula to Tralee, but he failed through lack of powder. Next year, however, Castlemaine fell after a blockade lasting for three months. Fitzmaurice tried to save it by bringing a band of Scottish mercenaries in from Thomond (Clare), but Perrot intercepted him, and drove him back to the fastness of Aherlow. Finally, under pressure from attacks from Sir Edmund Butler, who was working his passage back to favour, James Fitzmaurice, and his kinsman, the Seneschal of Imokilly, went to see Perrot at Kilmallock. There Perrot forced Fitzmaurice to lie prostrate on the flagstones of the church, 'taking the point of the Lord President's sword next to his heart, in token that he had received his life at the Queen's hands' and confessing his various treasons in Irish (**74, 26**).

James Fitzmaurice was partly induced to surrender because he had been profoundly disappointed by the lack of Spanish support for his rebellion. He had received a polite but vague reply to a memorial which he had sent to Philip II. The Spanish indecision was quite deliberate, and followed the line laid down in a memorandum in which Charles V had outlined Spanish policy towards Irish affairs. In this document it was maintained that the Desmonds should not be supported against the increasing power of the Tudor monarchy in Ireland. Apart from this, Spanish strength was already beginning to be sapped by the revolt of the Dutch 'sea-beggars' who had seized Brille in 1572 (**85, 84**).

In January 1573 the Earl of Desmond and his cousin Sir John of Desmond were permitted to return to Dublin. Desmond had been kept half-guest, half-prisoner in London since 1565. He had attempted to escape down the Thames with the help of Martin Frobisher, who was in fact acting as a double-agent on Burghley's behalf. When this ludicrous attempt to leave London was foiled Desmond tried another tack: he became an Anglican, swore to uphold the

Queen's peace, and solemnly promised not to exact tribute or otherwise molest the lesser lords living in his supremacy. Indeed, it now seemed that Desmond had become as tame and as much a Queen's man as either Ormond or Kildare (**6,** ch. xxx).

Perrot was most alarmed by Desmond's return to Ireland. He looked on him as fitter to keep Bedlam than to rule the newly reformed lands of Desmond. In despair, foreseeing the ruin of all his work in the pacification of Munster, he resigned, and set sail for England 'lamented by the poor, the widows, the feeble, and the unwarlike' (**26**). It was, however, only the close of Perrot's first appearance upon the stage of Elizabethan Ireland.

FLIGHT OF JAMES FITZMAURICE

As soon as Perrot's strong hand was removed fresh trouble broke out in Munster. James Fitzmaurice divorced his wife and married the widow of O'Connor Kerry, thus securing possession of Carrigafoyle castle, which commanded the southern shores of the wide estuary of the Shannon. Next, the Earl of Desmond escaped from his honourable confinement in Dublin at Hallowe'en 1573, and sought refuge with Rory Oge O'More of Leix. Rory was the leader of the O'Mores, who had been engaged in incessant frontier warfare ever since the confiscation and plantation of their territories under Mary. Together with his ally Fiach McHugh O'Byrne, chief of the unsubdued O'Byrnes of the Wicklow mountains, Rory was a constant reminder to the Dublin government and the citizens of how little 'civility' there was even on the borders of the Pale. Rory helped Desmond on his way to Limerick. There Desmond symbolically put on Irish dress, and from his castle at Askeaton announced the resumption of all claim to palatine jurisdiction in his lands in Kerry. Castlemaine was soon in Desmond hands again, and Fitzwilliam's administration in Dublin, lacking both money and resources, was powerless for the time being (**55**).

Kildare, Ormond and the Earl of Essex joined in negotiations with Desmond at Kilkenny, but without success. Indeed by July 1574 most of the Geraldines had decided to support Desmond in his resistance to royal authority, or encroachments on his lands or rights by the West Country adventurers. However, military action proved more effective than discussion, and Fitzwilliam and Ormond took

Derrinlaur castle near Clonmel, killing the entire garrison. Desmond, who detested such ruthlessness and preferred devious tergiversation, submitted at once, and surrendered his castles in Kerry.

The first phase of the Desmond rebellion in Munster ended in 1575. Early in the year James Fitzmaurice fled from Glin on the Shannon to St Malo in Brittany, and on 27 November Sir Peter Carew died. It was Carew's adventuring for land in Leinster and Munster which had led to the Desmond rebellion, in which James Fitzmaurice was the leading figure. So two major protagonists passed from the scene, one for ever, the other to reappear in 1579.

6 Fall of the Desmonds and the Plantation of Munster

> Oppression and extortion did maintain the greatness, and oppression and extortion did extinguish the greatness, of that house. Which may well be expressed by the old emblem of a torch turned downward with these words, 'Quod me alit, extinguit.'
>
> SIR JOHN DAVIES, *A Discovery of the True Causes why Ireland was never entirely subdued* . . . in (**21**), p. 309.

The flight of James Fitzmaurice Fitzgerald to France in 1575 and the death of the Earl of Essex in 1576 marked the end of the first phase of Elizabeth's reign in Ireland. Shane O'Neill's rebellion had demonstrated the breakdown of Henry VIII's policy of 'sober ways, politic drifts, and amiable persuasions' in dealing with the Gaelic lordships, while the years 1567–76 had witnessed attempts to establish settlements by Smith and Essex in Ulster and by Gilbert, Grenville and Carew in Munster, efforts marked in both cases by a contemptuous disregard for existing land titles. Inevitably this led to the fierce opposition of the O'Neills and the MacDonnells on the one hand, and of the Desmonds and MacCarthys on the other. Yet, by 1576 it was clear that the 'Enterprise of Ulster' had failed, while in Munster a course of events had been started which could only end in the downfall of the Geraldines of Desmond. Fitzmaurice's flight marked a half-way stage in this process. The return of Desmond to his estates had temporarily strengthened the Geraldines, and it began to be realized that the settlement of Munster was going to prove a protracted business. The whole problem, indeed, was no longer purely a domestic matter, but one involving the distinct possibility of foreign intervention. In this respect there was a close parallel with the revolt of the Netherlands against the imperial power of Spain (**85**).

THE RETURN OF FITZMAURICE

It was that stormy petrel, James Fitzmaurice, who made the Irish issue one of European importance. Admittedly, he had found nothing in France save fair words and empty promises since his arrival there in 1575. The Spanish, too, proved kind but unhelpful. Only in Rome did he receive a genuine welcome. Fitzmaurice saw himself as a crusader, leading a force of some 6000 men, officered by Spanish and Italian veterans, well armed and shriven by twenty priests, to free Ireland and save her from the Reformation. Pope Gregory XIII gave his sanction for a motley force of brigands and mercenaries to be raised. They were placed under the command of an extraordinary adventurer, Thomas Stukeley, a renegade Devonian. Stukeley had been licensed in 1562 to establish a colony in Florida, but had ended up instead in the more lucrative business of piracy off the Munster coast. Abandoning this he went to Spain, where Philip II knighted him and where he adopted the grandiose title of Duke of Ireland. He then went to Rome, and subsequently served against the Turks at the battle of Lepanto. This inconsequential adventurer was induced to allow the papal expeditionary force to serve with the King of Portugal in Morocco, where they were both killed in action in 1578. The remnant of Stukeley's force, amounting to about 600 men, was now offered to James Fitzmaurice, together with 6000 muskets, the whole to be transported to Ireland in two large and three smaller vessels (**6, 113**).

The administration pressed Sir Humphrey Gilbert's ships into service to oppose the landing of this little expedition. Gilbert's expedition to the West Indies had failed, and his seven vessels were lying off Dartmouth. They were made ready for sea, and Gilbert decided to intercept James Fitzmaurice by cruising off the coast of Galicia. However, he soon changed his mind, set course for Smerwick on the Dingle peninsula, and began cruising off the coast of Munster. One of his ships, the *Anne Aucher* was stationed as guardship in Kinsale. For these naval services Gilbert was paid £585 17*s* 7¾*d*, which he looked on as a niggardly recompense; to add to his difficulties the sailors made off with two of his ships and resumed their vocation as pirates (**67**, pp. 46–9). To crown all, James Fitzmaurice slipped through Gilbert's maritime net and his vessels cast anchor in Dingle harbour on 17 July 1579.

Fitzmaurice landed to seek provisions for his men. Having forced the port-reeve and citizens of Dingle to supply their wants, they set fire to the town, sailed round Slea Head, and established themselves on the northern shores of the Dingle peninsula at Smerwick harbour. There, on the promontory fort of Dun-an-Oir, they dug fresh entrenchments, and James Fitzmaurice issued a proclamation which made it clear that the rebellion was not against the 'lawful sceptre and honourable throne of England', but against the heretic Queen Elizabeth [**doc. 17**].

Elizabeth's sea power soon reasserted itself, and Fitzmaurice's shipping was attacked by Courtenay and Henry Davells. Davells later made his way down the entire length of the Dingle peninsula, and reconnoitred the Smerwick entrenchments. On his return he stayed at an inn in Tralee in company with Carter, the Provost Marshal of Munster. The inn was surrounded during the night by a party led by Sir John of Desmond, who was Davell's foster-brother. 'When Davells saw Sir John of Desmond enter his room with a drawn sword he called out, "What, son! what is the matter?" "No more son, nor no more father," said the other, "but make thyself ready for die thou shalt"' (**6,** ch. xxxvi). Carter was also murdered, and this deed went uncondemned by the undecided Earl of Desmond, who up to now had shown an equivocal attitude to the landing of James Fitzmaurice. Fitzmaurice, however, had no hesitation in condemning such a cowardly murder, and disowning the actions of Sir John of Desmond. Not long afterwards Fitzmaurice was killed in a minor skirmish with some of the Burkes. The comment of the *Four Masters* that, 'His death was the beginning of the decay of the honourable house of Desmond, out of which never issued so brave a man in all perfection, both for qualities of the mind and body, besides the league between him and others for the defence of religion' (**29**), may be supplemented by a tribute from his enemy, Sir John Perrot: 'He was a man very valiant, politicke and learned as any Rebell hath byn of that Nation for many Yeres.' (**26**).

PELHAM'S CAMPAIGN 1580

After James Fitzmaurice's ignominious end, Sir John of Desmond became the leader of the rebels in Munster. The Lord Justice, Sir William Drury, had only some 400 infantry and 200 horse to field against him. The Earl of Desmond still vacillated, and, on visiting the Lord Deputy's camp at Kilmallock, was quietly placed under arrest. Subsequently, he agreed to join in a half-hearted campaign in the counties of Limerick and Cork. Desmond's mind was made up for him by the appointment of the energetic Sir William Pelham as the new Lord Justice. He joined in rebellion with his kinsman, the Seneschal of Imokilly, and appeared under arms before the partly ruinous walls of Youghal. The mayor and some of the inhabitants had 'Desmond hearts', and on 15 November 1579, two days after Desmond had appeared, the town was entered and sacked. When eventually Youghal was recaptured by English forces under the command of the Earl of Ormond, the mayor was hanged in front of his own house for his supposed connivance (**6, 74**).

The decisive campaign began in 1580. Pelham's object was to make the Desmond lands 'as bare a country as ever Spaniard set foot in', a sentiment which clearly expressed the government's growing fear of a Spanish landing—a fear which haunted the 1580s and culminated in the ruthless execution carried out on the survivors of the Armada in 1588. Pelham marched from Limerick to Glin, whence Fitzmaurice had sailed in 1575, and thence into Kerry. There he laid waste the countryside from Listowel to Tralee. The Geraldine power was starting to crumble, for Lord Fitzmaurice submitted at Glin, and Patrick Fitzmaurice of Clanmaurice came in to make his peace at Lixnaw. Tralee was burned as a retribution for the murder of Davells and Carter, but progress down the mountainous spine of the Dingle peninsula was impeded by heavy snowfalls. Pelham therefore turned northwards to besiege Carrigafoyle on the Shannon estuary, which had become James Fitzmaurice's property by his second marriage. The castle was stormed by 1 April, the garrison killed, and, as the Desmond lands had now been split, their major centre of Askeaton surrendered [**doc. 20**] (**19**).

Pelham conferred with his associates at Limerick on 10 May, and decided to make another attempt to scour the remote Dingle peninsula. This time he marched from Askeaton to Castleisland in Kerry, 'a huge, monstrous castle of many rooms, but very filthy and full of cowdung'. Desmond and the papal nuncio, Dr Sanders, who had landed with Fitzmaurice at Dingle in 1579, managed to escape just in time. Some vestments, a sanctus bell, a lectern and a chalice cover, as well as the earl's barrels of whisky formed part of the spoil. 'Never was the bad earl and his legate *a latere* so bested in his own . . . county palatine of Kerry.' Curiously enough Desmond and Sanders distrusted one another, as well they might, for as the earl's fortunes sank, so the hopes of the nuncio rose. As an agent of the Counter-Reformation his concern was with the religious struggle of the age; he was naturally less interested in Desmond's desire to restore himself as a great Anglo-Irish lord (**51, 52**).

Pelham now marched from Castleisland to Castlemaine and on to Dingle. There they found Admiral Winter's ships safely anchored in the harbour, and the merchants' tower-houses ransacked, though still standing amidst the ruins of lesser homes. Pelham completed his campaign by returning to Castlemaine and Cork, where he summoned a meeting of all the Munster lords, at which they were all, with the exception of Lord Barrymore, received to the Queen's mercy. Pelham had every reason to be pleased with such a result of his campaign, even though his means of ending the Desmond rebellion had been as ruthless as those employed by Gilbert a decade earlier (**19**).

On 27 July 1580 Sir James of Desmond was captured by the Sheriff of Cork, Sir Cormac MacTeigue MacCarthy, and the earl himself was on the point of surrender when Lord Grey de Wilton, Pelham's successor as Lord Deputy arrived in August. The season was now drawing to a close, and on 5 September Admiral Winter sailed back to England, his sails and ropes rotted by the unceasing rain of a Kerry summer. A week later a body of 600 Italian troops with Spanish officers—survivors of the company originally raised by Thomas Stukeley—arrived at Smerwick.

THE MASSACRE OF SMERWICK

This Spanish and papal invading force carried with them 6000 stand of arms and four casks of money, and two emissaries of the Counter-Reformation: Dr Ryan, the catholic bishop of Killaloe, and Fr Matthew Oviedo, the apostolic commissary. Having entrenched themselves on the promontory fort at Smerwick, which had been refurbished by Fitzmaurice in the previous year, they marched down the Dingle peninsula and endeavoured to take the port of Fenit and the cathedral at Ardfert. They were repulsed by Ormond's men, and forced to retreat to Smerwick, a position which could not be taken without the use of artillery. Yet, since Winter had refitted and returned to Irish waters, and as the Lord Deputy and Walter Raleigh commanded a considerable body of seasoned troops, it was clear that Smerwick was garrisoned by doomed men.

Raleigh was Humphrey Gilbert's half-brother, and was related to the Grenvilles, Champernownes, Carews, Courtenays and St Legers who formed the bulk of the West Country adventurers in Munster.

He grew up in a world stirred by Hakluyt's *Voyages*, Drake's priva-
teering, Gilbert's propaganda for the North-West passage to Cathay
and his schemes for colonisation in Ireland. In 1580 Raleigh's
career began to open up with the opportunity of service in Ireland
with 'one hundred of those men presently levied in the City of
London . . . [and] . . . one cart, five post horses, and . . . convenient
shipping. (**69**).

> When Grey and Raleigh arrived opposite Smerwick they sent a
> trumpeter to the fort to ask who they might be, what was their
> business in Ireland, who had sent them, and why they had made
> a fortified place in Elizabeth's realm, and to bid them with
> all speed withdraw. They answered that they were sent, some by
> the most holy Father, the Pope of Rome, others by the Catholic
> King of Spain, to whom the Pope of Rome had granted Ireland,
> since Elizabeth had justly forfeited her right there by reason of her
> heresy.

The sappers were ordered to prepare trenches, guns were landed from
Winter's squadron and 'the soldiers meanwhile . . . set up their great
pieces for battery against the walls and both of them played for four
whole days against the fort'. The garrison attempted one or two
sallies against the siege works, but were driven back. Their hope lay
in effective help being sent to them by Desmond, but he proved a
broken reed. Accordingly, the Smerwick garrison asked for a parley.
The Lord Deputy refused to offer them any conditions of surrender,
so 'when they saw they could not prevail any way, then at length they
hanged out a white flag, and with one voice they all cried out:
'Misericordia! Misericordia! and offered to yield without any
conditions at all . . .' (**17,** p. 170). 'The Deputy, bitterly railing
against the Pope of Rome, bid them surrender themselves without
condition. And as they could obtain no other terms, they . . .
delivered themselves over to the mercy of the Deputy'.

Next morning the Spanish officers surrendered the fort, the troops
laid down their arms, the munitions, money and provender in the
fort were handed over, and then the Lord Deputy's decision that the
leaders should be spared and the rest put to the sword for an example,
and that any Irish found in the fort should be hanged, was put into
speedy effect: 'Then put I in certain bands, who straight fell to
execution. There were six hundred slain' (**18, 69, 74**). Such was the
massacre of Smerwick, ably carried out, on Grey's orders, by Walter

Raleigh and Captain Mackworth. This appalling event was an indication of how much the government feared the possibility of foreign intervention in Ireland. It was in the merciless tradition of the 'Pardon of Maynooth', and was the result of a weak administration, habitually starved of proper resources, faced with what was felt to be a dangerous combination of 'malice domestic and foreign levy'. The excuse proffered that it was impossible to dispose of so many prisoners other than by summary execution holds little credibility, for not only were ships available to transport them, but their potential allies, the Desmond rebels, were by this stage no longer a menace. In January, Sir John of Desmond was killed in a chance encounter, and in November 1583 the Earl of Desmond himself was killed in Glenageenty in the hills above Tralee by one of the O'Moriarty's, whose cattle his men had stolen, and whose wife and children had been shamefully treated. Such was the sordid end of the noble house of Desmond (**6,** chs. xxxviii and xxxix).

THE PLANTATION OF MUNSTER

The death of the Earl of Desmond removed the last obstacle in the pathway of the Elizabethan adventurers in Munster, and to the desire of the administration to reduce the whole province to English law and 'civility'. There were two aspects of life there, both of which were described by the poet, Edmund Spenser. One was the devastation and misery caused by such a prolonged period of warfare and uncertainty reaching back to 1565-9; the other was the fundamental attractiveness and potential richness of the province as a colonial plantation [**doc. 28**]. In 1586 the parliament summoned by Sir John Perrot, the Lord Deputy, laid the foundation for this new Utopia by passing an Act for the confiscation of the vast Desmond estates, by which 'all and singular the said honours, castles, manors, messuages, lands, tenements, rents, reversions, remainders, possessions, rights, conditions, interests, offices, fees, annuities, and all other their hereditaments, goods, chattels, debts, and other things . . . shall be deemed, vested, and judged to be in the actual and real possession of your Majesty' (**17,** pp. 241–2).

The confiscated lands were divided up into seignories of 12,000, 8,000, 6,000, and 4,000 acres. In addition bogs, heaths and waste were included as commons in each undertaker's holding, and were not subject to quit-rent to the Crown. Undertakers were encouraged to settle in Munster by the financial inducements of freedom from cesses and other impositions, and freedom to export produce from their estates without payment of duty for five years. The plantation, like that of Leix and Offaly, was designed to exclude the 'mere' Irish and to follow up Sir Thomas Smith's and Humphrey Gilbert's concepts by encouraging the settlement of English undertakers. In particular, and this again is reminiscent of Smith's propaganda about the Ards, younger sons were invited to consider become undertakers, for there they were told, they could become great lords [**doc. 29**] (**17,** pp. 243–5). Nevertheless, the plantation of Munster failed to take root, and was largely swept away in the uprising in 1598. It failed because there was a lack of careful planning, a lack of a proper cross-section of the population in the plantation, and because nothing was done to prevent an adventurer like Raleigh from acquiring enormous holdings, which could not be either properly settled or exploited. It formed a striking contrast to the later plantation of Ulster and settlement of Antrim and Down, which made a permanent mark on Irish history (**36, 25**).

7 The Settlement of Connacht

Fortuna favet fortibus — motto of the O'Flahertys.

West of the Shannon the province of Connacht had been left largely under the local rule of its hibernicised Anglo-Irish and Gaelic lords by the Dublin administration. But with the Desmond rebellion in Munster on the one hand, and the greater part of Ulster unsubdued on the other, government policy began to favour more active intervention, with the twin objects of spreading acceptance of the rule of English law and of securing the province from Spanish or Scottish intervention. At the same time the problems of Connacht were less urgent than those in Ulster or Munster, for it was remote from the capital, and had a sparse population and few natural resources (**2, 13**).

King John had made a grant of Connacht to William de Burgo in 1205, but before the latter could take possession of his fief he died, and it was left to his son Richard de Burgo to conquer the province in 1235. Richard took the title 'Dominus Connaciae', lording it over such subtenants as the Stauntons, Prendergasts, and the Berminghams of Athenry, but leaving Roscommon to the O'Connors, the Gaelic 'kings' of Connacht, and the hills and glens of Leitrim to the O'Rourkes. The Norman families in the west of Ireland soon became hibernicised, and intermarried with the O'Briens and the O'Connors, and by the end of the thirteenth century it was clear that the result of the Norman penetration into Connacht was a draw (**3, 5**).

In 1264 Walter de Burgo, Lord of Connacht, became Earl of Ulster, and under his son Richard de Burgo, the 'Red Earl' (1280–1326), the power of the Anglo-Normans reached its height. With the murder of William de Burgo, the 'Brown Earl' in 1333 'at the ford of Carrickfergus', the link between Ulster and Connacht was broken. In Connacht power passed to two junior branches of the de Burgo family, who gaelicised their surname to Burke and adopted brehon law. These were the MacWilliam Burkes of Mayo (lower Connacht), and the Clanrickard Burkes of Galway (upper Connacht). In the fifteenth century the Clanrickard Burkes made a marriage alliance

61

with the Geraldine house of Kildare, as did the princely O'Neills of Tyrone (see chapter 1), and under the policy of 'surrender and regrant' Ulick Burke became Earl of Clanrickard, just as O'Brien became Earl of Thomond.

These new titles provided a link with the larger world represented by the Tudor monarchy. Another was provided by the port and town of Galway, the great emporium of the west. Established in the thirteenth century, it was dominated by a merchant class composed of families of Norman descent. The Martins, Blakes, Lynches, Joyces, Kirwans, ffrenches and others were collectively known as the 'tribes of Galway' and were ferociously determined to keep the native Irish outside the town walls: 'neither 'O' nor 'Mac' shall strut or swagger through the streets of Galway'. The merchant families were rich and 'great adventurers at sea', their wealth resting on trade with Spain. Wine was imported in such quantities that Galway's economic hinterland extended eastwards across the midlands as far as Meath. The wine trade was exempted from payment of the tax or prisage on wines which had been granted to the Butlers of Ormond by King John, and this valuable exemption was not lost until 1584 (**40**).

Galway itself was but a small town, but had 'fair and stately buildings, the fronts of the houses (being) all of hewed stone up to the top, garnished with fair battlements in a uniform course'. The town was built upon rock and firm ground beside the river Corrib and the sea, and 'compassed with a strong wall and good defences, after the ancient manner, and such as with a reasonable garrison may defend itself against an enemy'. Municipal government was in the hands of a mayor and two bailiffs, who were elected by the 'sovereign, provost, bailiffs and commonalty of the town'. The charter of 1549 expressly provided that civic freedom should be upheld against the MacWilliam Burke, lord of Clanrickard, who 'should have no authority in the town', and that all vessels entering the port should pay tolls to the town authorities. Finally, the mayor, bailiffs and commonalty were given freedom to export any merchandise they pleased from the town; their liberties were to be modelled on those granted by charter to the town of Drogheda, just as those of Dublin were similar to those granted to Bristol; 'saving to the King, the rents . . . and other profits which were accustomed to be rendered out of said town' (**33, 41, 40, 17,** pp. 365–8).

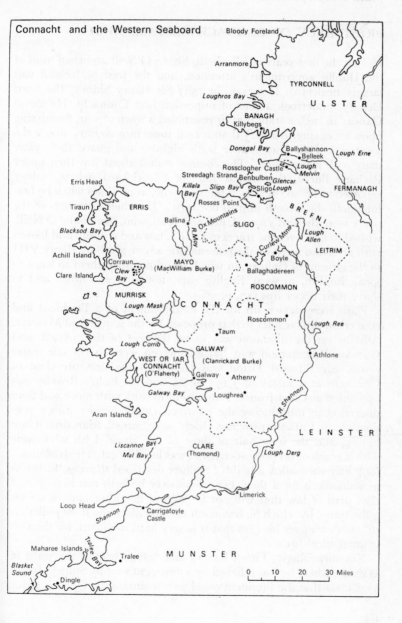

Connacht and the Western Seaboard

Bloody Foreland
Arranmore
TYRCONNELL
Loughros Bay
ULSTER
BANAGH
Killybegs
Donegal Bay
Ballyshannon
Belleek
Lough Erne
Rossclogher Castle
Lough
Melvin
Streedagh Strand
Benbulben
Glencar
FERMANAGH
Erris Head
Killala
Bay
Sligo Bay
Sligo
Lough
BREFNI
Tiraun
ERRIS
Rosses Point
Blacksod Bay
Ballina
Ox Mountains
SLIGO
R. Moy
Lough
Allen
Achill Island
Corraun
Curlew Mtns
LEITRIM
Clare Island
Clew
Bay
MAYO
(MacWilliam Burke)
Boyle
Ballaghadereen
ROSCOMMON
MURRISK
Lough Mask
C O N N A C H T
Roscommon
Lough Ree
Lough Corrib
Taum
GALWAY
Athlone
WEST OR IAR
CONNACHT
(O'Flaherty)
(Clanrickard Burke)
Galway
Athenry
Galway Bay
Loughrea
LEINSTER
Aran Islands
R. Shannon
Liscannor Bay
Mal Bay
CLARE
(Thomond)
Lough Derg
Loop Head
Limerick
Shannon
Carrigafoyle
Castle
Maharee Islands
Blasket
Sound
Tralee Bay
Tralee
M U N S T E R
Dingle

0   10   20   30 Miles

PRESIDENCY OF CONNACHT ESTABLISHED

During the first years of Elizabeth, Shane O'Neill absorbed most of the Dublin government's attention, and the west of Ireland was largely neglected. However, in 1567 Sir Henry Sidney, the Lord Deputy, undertook a tour of inspection into Connacht. He found Galway in such a state that 'it resembled a town of war, frontiering upon an enemy, [rather] than a civil town in a country under the sovereign. They watch their walls nightly, and guard their gates daily with armed men.' The country round about was then under Richard Burke, the second Earl of Clanrickard, whom Sidney reported to be 'so ruled by a putative wife, as oft times when he best intendeth she forceth him to do worst'. The chief disturbers of the peace were the earl's sons, Ulick and John, who, like Shane O'Neill, wished to kick over the traces of English law and custom, and looked with profound scorn on the paternalistic advice given by Henry VIII to the citizens of Galway, in which he admonished them to learn to speak English, to wear English caps, not to wear saffron and to shave their upper lips (**17,** p. 366).

Plans were drawn up for the establishment of a President and council on similar lines to that proposed for the province of Munster. Athlone on the Shannon was to be the seat of the council, and Galway, Roscommon and Ballaghadereen were to become assize towns. Sir Edward Fitton was chosen as the first president of Connacht at a salary of £133 6s 8d, and Sir Ralph Rokeby was appointed as Chief Justice. Fitton went to work with more zeal than discretion in introducing the reformed church service into a pre-dominantly Catholic province. 'Idols' were burned, friars driven into hiding, and the long hair of those of the 'mere' Irish who came within reach of his provost-marshal was forcibly cut. The Irishman's long hair was called a 'glibb'; Spenser described them as 'fit masks as a mantle is for a thief. For whensoever he hath run himself into that peril of law that will not be known, he either cutteth off his glibb quite, by which he becometh nothing like himself, or pulleth it so low down over his eyes that it is very hard to discern his thievish countenance' (**21**).

Not surprisingly, Fitton had to take refuge behind the walls of Galway, where he was relieved by a force sent west by Sidney. It was soon clear that the President could only maintain the Queen's peace within the range of his small force of musketeers. Accordingly the Earl of Clanrickard was released from detention in Dublin and sent back to Connacht with a commission to restore order and grant pardons under the Great Seal. This proved temporarily effective, for, as the earl reported: 'I did within a twelvemonth hang my own son, my brother's son, my cousin-german's son . . . besides fifty of my own followers that bare armour and weapons.' Meantime Fitton was cooped up in the castle at Athlone, from which he impotently observed the increasing anarchy in Connacht. Athlone town itself was attacked and burnt and soon after this humiliation Fitton abandoned his post, thus confessing the absolute failure of his mission (**6**).

During Sidney's second term of office as Lord Deputy (1575–77) a fresh look was taken at the tangled problems of Connacht. The former O'Brien territory of Thomond, where the earl 'hath neither wit of himself to govern, nor grace or capacity to learn of others', was erected into the county of Clare. 'Thus much for Thomond, a limb of Munster, but in my last government here annexed to the President of Connaught by the name of the county of Clare' (**18**). Sidney next proceeded to divide Connacht into the counties of Sligo, Mayo, Galway and Roscommon. This was an important extension of English law and administration, bringing both the hibernicised lords like MacWilliam Burke of Mayo, and Gaelic lords like the O'Connors of Roscommon and Sligo into the network of sheriffs and county administration. In Galway the Earl of Clanrickard's sons, Ulick and John Burke submitted to Sidney. They 'came into the church . . . on a Sunday at public service, and there craved their pardon. I committed them to my marshal, and have them here prisoners in this castle of Dublin' (**40**). Following this the various septs of the Clanrickard Burkes made their submission, as did the O'Flahertys of west Connacht. The Bermingham town of Athenry, which had been burned by the earl's sons ('college, parish church, and all that was there . . . yet the mother of one of them was buried in that church'), was rebuilt, and several castles garrisoned for the Queen. In short, when Sidney reached Athlone he appeared to have settled Connacht; he even thought that the province would become financially self-supporting within eighteen months (**19**). The fragile nature of Sidney's settlement was dramatically illuminated by the escape of John and Ulick Burke from their confinement in Dublin: 'albeit they were mortal enemies (though brethren), yet *in odium* *tertiae*, *nempe*, the Queen, and English government, they conjured and joined in actual rebellion, shaking off and cutting in pieces their English garments upon the river of Shannon' (**19, 29**).

THE GOVERNORSHIP OF SIR NICHOLAS MALBY

In September 1576 Sidney appointed Sir Nicholas Malby as military governor of Connacht, so indicating his acceptance of the fact that the province was not yet ready for the primarily civil administration of a president and council. Philip Sidney, then aged twenty-two, being a young man of 'sufficiency, honesty, virtue and zeal' was ordered to join Malby's staff. Malby wasted no time in dealing with the main problems that faced him. First, he carried out a ruthless campaign in Clare against the earl's sons and their followers, with the main object of stamping out the incessant intrigues between them and the Desmond rebels in Munster. Secondly, he turned to deal with the Scots in Mayo. The key castle of Sligo was first secured, thus closing the gateway to north-west Ulster. Then O'Connor Sligo and O'Rourke of Leitrim pledged themselves to try to keep the Scots out. Thirdly, Malby struck a blow on the western seaboard at the O'Malleys, who had been renowned for generations as seamen, and who dominated Clew bay and Achill island. Their chief was Grania O'Malley, who as 'Granuaile' became a legend in her lifetime. She was born about 1530, daughter to Dubhdara O'Malley, the chief of Murrisk in Mayo. She first married one of the O'Flahertys, and her second husband was Richard Burke, nicknamed Richard-in-Iron. With him she repaired to Galway to meet Sidney in 1576. The Lord Deputy was much impressed, describing her as 'a most famous feminine sea captain . . . [who] offered her service with three galleys and 200 fighting men either in Ireland or Scotland; she brought with her her husband, for she was as well by sea as by land more than Mrs Mate with him; he was of the nether Burkes, and now as I hear MacWilliam Eochtar, and called by nickname Richard-in-Iron' (**74, 40, 41**).

Sir Nicholas Malby attacked one of the O'Malley castles on Clew bay with typical ruthlessness: 'I put the band [i.e. the garrison of the castle], both men, women and children to the sword whereupon all the other castles in the country were given up without any resistance' (**6**). Grania O'Malley surrendered to Malby, but her husband sought refuge among the many islands of Clew bay. Malby commandeered boats on Achill Island, and in the maritime campaign which followed over 100 of Richard Burke's followers died of starvation. Finally Richard Burke submitted.

Malby's stern action against the O'Malleys was partly dictated by fear of fresh Scottish incursions, for the O'Malleys sometimes hired gallowglasses, and partly by the alarm caused by James Fitzmaurice's activities on the continent. So, to secure the western coasts, the *Lion*, the *Dreadnought* and the *Swiftsure* were provisioned, and sent to cruise off Mayo and Galway. The *Handmaid* was ordered to join those vessels later, when she had completed her commission to 'transport or waft the treasure and munition now to be sent' (**19**).

For a year or two an uneasy peace prevailed. However, in 1581 a band of 600 Scots invaded Connacht to help Richard-in-Iron against his kinsman Richard MacOliver Burke. Malby's men drove them back to the river Moy, and they were subsequently forced to retreat back to Ulster. Malby now decided to turn the poachers into gamekeepers by appointing Richard-in-Iron as the MacWilliam (the chief of the Mayo Burkes), and Shane MacOliver Burke as sheriff of co. Mayo. Soon after this the old Earl of Clanrickard died in 1582, laying a curse upon his two sons Ulick and John if they should ever again prove disobedient subjects. Ulick, the elder son, succeeded to the title as third Earl of Clanrickard, and his brother John became Baron of Leitrim. It was not long before the hostility of these two brothers was stilled for ever, for John was murdered and the new earl underwent a 'sea-change' into a prop of such law and order in Galway as there was. Finally, Malby himself died in March 1584, and the annalists lamented his passing with this epitaph: 'There came not to Erin in his own time, or often before, a better gentleman of the Foreigners than he, and he placed all Connacht under bondage' (**29**).

SIR JOHN PERROT AND THE COMPOSITION OF CONNACHT

Just as the end of the Desmond rebellion in Munster in 1583 opened up the way for the plantation of Munster, so the successes of Malby's military regime in Connacht provided the opportunity for introducing a more settled and orderly pattern of life into that province.

Main Developments

It fell to Sir John Perrot to return to Ireland as Lord Deputy to preside over the period of less than five years between Desmond's death and the crisis of the Spanish Armada. Sir John arrived in Ireland in June 1584, and at once addressed himself to the installation of Sir John Norris as Lord President of Munster, and Sir Richard Bingham as Malby's successor in Connacht (**6,** ch. xl). Having done this Perrot turned to deal with the Scots in Ulster, who were looked upon as alien intruders into the realm, and who played a continually disturbing role as mercenaries in Connacht.

With a force of 2,000 men, some of whom had been raised by the traditional expedient of a hosting of the 'Englishry' at Tara in Meath, Perrot marched northwards to face a force of some 4,000 Scots. But, this was not, as Perrot thought, an orthodox invasion, but a raid for cattle from Tyrconnell. Perrot, therefore, found nobody to fight, and, to add to his frustration, his ships failed to intercept the Scottish galleys. It was, accordingly, some compensation to him when he captured the MacDonnell castle of Dunluce. This was a sore blow to Sorley Boy MacDonnell, who had reappeared in Ireland after a decade of exile in Scotland. Sorley retreated once more to Scotland to seek help from his kinsmen. It was a frustrating campaign for Perrot. He had failed to expel or crush the Scots, and the Queen rubbed salt in the wound, by writing, 'I know you do nothing but with a good intention for my service, but yet take better heed ere you use us so again' (**6, 26, 59**).

In the late autumn of 1584 a force of 1,300 Scots landed in Rathlin, and subsequently attacked Sir Henry Bagenal who was encamped at Red Bay. They were repulsed, and withdrew to Ballycastle, where a sharp but indecisive skirmish took place in early January 1585. Perrot rightly blamed the lack of men and money for this unsatisfactory result, but began to feel more hopeful when Sorley Boy sought to parley, saying that he wished to settle down in Ulster as a law-abiding subject of Queen Elizabeth. But Sorley's terms for the settlement were too high, and so Perrot once more chased him off to Scotland (**6, 59,** ch. iv *passim*). Once more the game of hide-and-seek was repeated, for the Scots returned to Antrim in August 1585 and recaptured Dunluce. Perrot was furious at seeing his work so easily overthrown, for it confirmed the MacDonnell hold on north Antrim. Nevertheless, he was realist enough to invite Sorley Boy to Dublin, where the old chieftain made his submission to the Crown. He was granted most of the Glens of Antrim and the Route, and was appointed constable of Dunluce castle. With his submission ended the Elizabethan attempt to extirpate the Scots from Ulster, and in this was laid the foundation of the later earldom of Antrim (**6, 59**). It was left to Bingham to deal with the Scots in Connacht.

In 1585 Perrot summoned the third and most important parliament of Elizabeth's reign. The parliament of 1560 had been summoned to pass the measures required for the establishment of the reformed religion in Ireland, namely, the Acts of Uniformity and Supremacy. Sidney's parliament of 1569–70 had been chiefly noted for the act for the attainder of Shane O'Neill, the passage of a subsidy bill, and the emergence of an Anglo-Irish opposition to the government of Ireland, which had by this time passed completely into the hands of the English by birth. Perrot's parliament was more representative than that of 1560, an index of how far the extension of English law over Ireland had progressed since that time. There was an increase in the county representation from 20 to 27, and in the borough representation from 29 to 36. The bulk of the M.P.s were Anglo-Irish stock, with only a thin sprinkling of 'mere' Irish members. In addition, the more recent settlers, such as Sir Warham St Leger or Sir Richard Bingham, formed a significant minority of the Commons. Perrot insisted that all the members should come to parliament attired in English clothes: 'The better to encourage them herto, the Lord Deputy bestowed both Gownes and Cloakes of Velvet and Satten on some of them'. At the opening of parliament in Dublin those who observed the Lord Deputy remarked that they 'never beheld a Man of such Comeliness in Countenance, Gesture, Gate, and other Features, as he appeared to be in his Parliament Robes' (**26**). Yet, beneath this impressive parliamentary splendour there lay the makings of a distinct 'country party' in opposition to the government. Religious grievances existed but did not dominate, although it can truly be suggested that the erosion of the loyalty of the catholic Anglo-Irish had already begun (**108**). Then there were constitutional grievances such as the proposal to replace the time-honoured cess in the Pale with a tax on ploughlands and the imposition of a Speaker nominated by the Lord Deputy: underneath lay the basic grievance of the Anglo-Irish at their exclusion from any real share in the government (**108**). A strange paradox was the opposition to the government's proposal to suspend Poynings' Law, for it was now looked upon by the Anglo-Irish as a safeguard against the hasty introduction of measures which they disliked. Parliament was prorogued in May 1585, and met for its second session in April 1586. The second session was primarily concerned with the attainder of the late Earl of Desmond, the necessary legal basis for the plantation of Munster. Three weeks after reassembling this parliament was dissolved (**6, 108, 95**). Soon afterwards a composition for cess was arranged with the gentry of the Pale, an indication that, from the government's point of view, it was easier to achieve results outside parliament.

Perrot's greatest success during this difficult period of office lay in the settlement of Connacht. Commissioners were appointed to look into the affairs of that province, and to 'call before them all the nobility, spiritual and temporal, and all the chieftains and lords of the countries, and thereupon, in lieu of the uncertain cess borne to us, and of the cuttings and spendings of the lords, compound for a rent certain to us, upon every quarter or quantity of land within the province' (**17**, p. 162). Sir Richard Bingham, who had succeeded Malby, was appointed chief commissioner, together with the Earl of Thomond, the Earl of Clanrickard, the Baron of Athenry, Sir Turlough O'Brien, Sir Richard Burke (Richard-in-Iron), The O'Connor Don, The O'Rourke and The O'Flaherty. The commissioners travelled through the entire province assessing the size of land holdings, and establishing specific rents for each, as well as reserving certain sums to the Crown. It was reckoned that by this composition the Crown would gain some £4,000 per annum, in addition to various other escheats and royalties (**22**) [**doc. 12**]. This composition may be compared to the arrangements reached in 1591 with the MacMahons of Monaghan, by which the position and income of the local landlords was secured. It was an expedient method of securing stability in a large area, and was simpler and cheaper than the complex processes of confiscation and plantation. Had Connacht been as fruitful, populous and accessible as Munster, the course of events would doubtless have been quite different.

It now remained only for Sir Richard Bingham to enforce law and order in Connacht. This involved dealing with ordinary malefactors, as at the assizes held in Galway after which seventy were hanged, 'cutting off a few bad members' (**40, 41**), and dealing the Scottish mercenaries a crushing blow. They landed in Inishowen in northern Tyrconnell, and crossing the river Erne at Belleek, passed Bingham's outposts in the Curlew mountains by night. They continued their march into Mayo, but Bingham was just as swift and caught them near Ballina: 'About one of the clock we did join battle, and they did set their backs to the great river called the Moy, and the Governor (Sir R. Bingham) and we that were but a small number did with him ... charge them ... so that they could not pass our foot battle, and there God be thanked, we did drown and kill ... about the number of a thousand or eleven hundred ... (**17,** pp. 210–11). This victory of Bingham's put an end to the Scottish incursions into Connacht. It completed a process of extending law and order over the west of Ireland which had been begun by Sir Henry Sidney twenty years earlier. The plantation of Munster and the composition of Connacht meant that English law and administration was now complete over those two provinces, a fact of which the survivors of the Armada were to become painfully aware in 1588.

8 The Spanish Armada and Ireland

MARINERS: All lost! to prayers, to prayers! all lost!

GONZALO: Now would I give a thousand furlongs of sea
for an acre of barren ground; long heath,
brown furze, anything;
The wills above be done! but I would fain die
a dry death.

W. SHAKESPEARE, *The Tempest*, I, i.

On 13 August 1588 the Spanish fleet lay abreast of the Firth of Forth, watching the withdrawal of the English ships to the south. Seven ships of the line had been lost in the Channel fighting, and most vessels had been drubbed by English culverins. One-fifth of Medina Sidonia's men had been killed or disabled, and food and water were running low. Orders were now issued to the fleet for the long voyage home to Spain. The fleet was to clear the Shetlands, to steer out into the Atlantic north-west of Rockall, giving Ireland a wide berth 'for fear of the harm that may happen to you upon that coast'. The Armada altered course to WSW on 21 August, and for the next three weeks encountered gales and headwinds coming from that quarter. By early September some of the ships had parted company with the main fleet, and the tale of disaster on the Irish coasts began (**83, 74, 27**).

The immediate crisis in Ireland caused by the Spanish Armada did not last more than six weeks. Towards the end of August, Fitzwilliam and his administration became aware that the Spanish fleet was sailing north-west round the British Isles. Fitzwilliam justly complained that his lot was hard, 'who in so . . . troublesome a time, bearing the weighty burthen of this government over a people for the most part by nature rebellious, and contemners of all godliness, have nevertheless neither men nor almost any money to make account of if cause of service should fall forth' (**18**). This lack of adequate resources for defence against a possible Spanish landing goes far to explain the ruthlessness towards those who did struggle ashore, and to those who endeavoured to help them.

SHIPWRECKS ON THE WESTERN SEABOARD

The extent of the Spanish disaster was not at first apparent. Rumour filled the air and reports of specific wrecks only came in piecemeal. For example, Dominic Rice, the Sovereign of Dingle, reported the presence of the Spanish vessels in the Blasket Sound, adding that 'a Scotchman taken prisoner by them reports them sick, destitute of victual, and in great extremity'. The Mayor of Limerick reported eleven ships in the Shannon, and suggested that as many as 140 ships of the Armada had been beaten by the weather to the Irish coast. By 10 September the Attorney General, Sir John Popham, provided Burghley with a summary of the situation:

> The advertisements are that on Thursday last and sithence that time, there arrived first a bark which wrecked at the Bay of Tralee another great ship being now also near that place. After that two great ships and one frigate at the Blaskets in the Sound there, seven other sail in the Shannon by Carrigafoyle, whereof two are taken to be of a thousand tons apiece, two more of 400 tons the piece, and three small barks. At Loop Head four great ships and toward the Bay of Galway four great ships more (**18, 6,** ch. xlii), [**doc. 21**].

The Spanish Armada suffered its worst losses in Ireland. Only two of the vessels which made for the western seaboard in search of provisions, water and an opportunity to patch up their hulls, managed to get away (**83**). One of them was the *San Juan*, fifty guns, of the squadron of Portugal, commanded by Juan Martin de Recalde, Knight of Santiago and Admiral of the Armada, who had commanded the right wing of the Spanish crescent formation in the Channel. The *San Juan* had been pounded by Drake in the *Revenge*, Hawkins in the *Victory* and Frobisher in the *Triumph*. She had been mauled but not put out of action; now her commander had brought her safely to waters with which he was familiar, for it was he who had commanded the ships of the Smerwick expedition in 1580. Recalde's men were desperately short of food and water, and a message was sent to the Sovereign of Dingle asking for provisions. However, he offered no assistance, and Recalde secured what he needed for his ships by force, some of his men being taken prisoner. He also embarked the survivors of the *Santa Maria de la Rosa* and the *San Juan de Ragusa*, which had foundered off the Blaskets. Recalde

73

managed to reach Corunna on 7 October, and not long afterwards he died, worn out by his exertions. In all this Recalde had shown considerable seamanship in making a landfall off the Blaskets, in anchoring in a sound where he was sheltered from all winds save that which would blow his vessels homewards, and in securing water and victuals for his men.

The merchantman *Trinidad* was probably wrecked on the Maharee Islands in Tralee Bay; certainly a small vessel—a *zabra*—with a crew of twenty-four was wrecked, and the crew surrendered to Lady Denny of Tralee. She ordered them all to be executed as 'there was no safe keeping for them'; this, in spite of the fact that three of them offered ransoms for their lives, saying that they had friends in Waterford to redeem them, as well they might, for some of this ship's company were Biscayans, a people who had long been involved in trading to the Irish ports (**27, 74, 94, 99**).

In Clare the sheriff, Boethius Clancy, was equally ruthless. Two large galleons were wrecked in Mal Bay, one of which may have been the transport *San Esteban*. Another, the galleass *Zuniga* ran for shelter to Liscannor Bay, and sent one of her cockboats ashore for water and food; 'it is not our English cockboats; it would carry twenty men at least, and it is painted red, with the red anchor . . .' (**19**). The *Zuniga* eventually reached Le Havre, having lost eighty men. The survivors from the two galleons were all executed on Clancy's orders. To sum up, so far as is known 'not one Spaniard escaped in Munster', an indication of how effectively the law was now enforced in that subdued province (**94**).

In Connacht the Governor, Sir Richard Bingham, exercised 'great care and travail which . . . kept the Spaniards from all kind of relief'. A proclamation was issued that every man should bring any Spanish prisoners he might have within four hours to the Justices of the Peace on pain of death. Accordingly some 300 survivors from two large transports which had been wrecked in Galway Bay were brought prisoner to Galway and there executed on Bingham's orders (**94, 40, 42**). However, not all the inhumanity to the Armada survivors stemmed from official orders, as was illustrated by the fate of the crew of the *Gran Grin*, 1160 tons, which drifted into Clew Bay in a sinking condition. One hundred of her complement managed to land on Clare Island, an O'Malley stronghold. The wreck then drifted across the mouth of the bay, and struck on the rocks of the Curraun peninsula, near Achill Island. 'The same ship is cast upon the shore and past recovery. . . . There is come ashore of them 16 persons alive with their chains of gold, and apprehended in the hands of a tenant of my Lord of Ormond.' Meanwhile the Spaniards on Clare Island tried to escape in some of the local fishing boats (currachs), but the islanders, led by their chieftain, Dubhdara Ruadh O'Malley, attacked them and all the Spaniards were killed, including Don Pedro de Mendoza, their commander (**43**).

Erris Head and the cliffs of north Mayo presented a navigational hazard to the Spanish ships, a hazard not lessened by the charts of the period, which failed to show the proper western extension of that portion of the coast. 'Eight of the ships known to have been caught by this trap were lost, and possible others were dashed against the iron-bound Mayo shore, of which no records exist' (**99**). Several ships sought refuge in Blacksod Bay. Indeed, at one stage it was rumoured that the Duke of Medina Sidonia himself had been lost in a galleon off Tiraun; more certainly it was in Blacksod Bay that the corpse of Maurice Fitzgerald, son of James Fitzmaurice Fitz- gerald, was 'cast into the sea with great solemnity'. There, too, came the Levant galleon *La Rata Coronada*, 820 tons and thirty-five guns commanded by Don Alonso de Leyva. Don Alonso had commanded the squadron of Levant galleons on the left wing of the Armada in the Channel, and had the honour of being engaged by Lord Thomas Howard of Effingham himself. His ship was joined in Blacksod bay by *La Nuestra Senora de Begona*, and *La Duquesa Santa Ana*. Unhappily, de Leyva's ship dragged her anchor and grounded by 11 September, so he and his men landed and fortified themselves in a castle on shore. Subsequently, de Leyva joined forces with the people from *La Duquesa Santa Ana*, and dug themselves in at Tiraun castle. *La Duquesa Santa Ana* was patched up, and de Leyva and his crews sailed northwards until they reached Loughros Bay in Donegal, where they were again shipwrecked. The ship's company scrambled ashore and made their way across country to Killybegs, an excellent natural harbour in the territory of MacSweeny Banagh, who was prepared to help the Armada survivors. Earlier three Spanish ships had made for Killybegs, but 'one of them was cast away a little with- out the harbour, another running aground on the shore brake to pieces. The third being a galley, and sore bruised with the seas, was repaired in the said harbour with some of the planks of the second ship.' This was the *Girona*, one of four Neapolitan galleasses, which had served under Don Hugo de Moncada, and was a sister ship of

75

the *Zuniga*, which had limped home back to Le Havre. Undaunted, Alonso de Leyva and his men sailed from Killybegs on 16 October bound for the Western Isles of Scotland. Two days later the *Girona* struck on the rocky shores of the Giant's Causeway, and the whole company save five perished [**doc. 21**]. When this news reached Philip II in the Escorial it was remarked that he felt more grief for the death of Don Alonso de Leyva than for the loss of the fleet. Sorley Boy Mac-Donnell salvaged some butts of wine from the wreck and mounted some of her guns in Dunluce castle. The survivors he protected and sent across to comparative safety in neutral Scotland (**43, 99**).

CAPTAIN CUELLAR'S ADVENTURES

Twenty Spanish captains had been tried as scapegoats by Medina Sidonia after the passage of the Channel and the retreat from Gravelines. One had been hanged from the yardarm of a despatch-boat (*zabra*) and sent round the fleet *pour encourager les autres*; the other captains had been relieved of their commands and placed in the custody of the Judge Advocate General, Don Martin de Aranda. Among them was Don Francisco de Cuellar, captain of the *San Pedro*, twenty-four guns, a galleon of the Castile squadron. Cuellar angrily protested that his mate had pulled the *San Pedro* out of the formation in order to carry out repairs; his death sentence was commuted, although he had to remain with the Judge Advocate on board his ship, a large Levanter. This vessel, accompanied by two others (one of which was probably the *San Juan de Sicilia* commanded by Don Diego Enriquez), was driven back from Blacksod Bay in co. Mayo to seek shelter near Rosses Point in co. Sligo. However, some days later a storm blew up which drove the vessels ashore on Streedagh strand. About a thousand of the Spaniards were lost:

> Many were drowning within the ships; others, casting themselves into the water, sank to the bottom without returning to the surface; others on rafts and barrels, and gentlemen on pieces of timber; others cried aloud in the ships, calling upon God; captains threw their chains and crown pieces into the sea; the waves swept others away, washing them out of the ships . . . the land and shore were full of enemies . . . when any one of our people reached the beach, two hundred savages and other enemies fell upon him and stripped him of what he had on until he was left in his naked skin.

Cuellar managed to reach the shore, though de Aranda was drowned in spite of his efforts to save him. Next day began Cuellar's extraordinary odyssey. First, he returned to the beach where he gave Don Diego Enriquez an honourable burial. Then he was attacked and stripped of his belongings, including the 45 crowns he had received as his payment in advance at Corunna, and some holy relics, which were taken by one of his attackers, a 'savage damsel', who 'hung them around her neck, making me a sign that she wished to keep them, saying to me that she was a Christian: which she was in like manner as Mahomet' [**doc. 4**]. After this Cuellar slowly and painfully continued his journey, passing Ben Bulben and the Dartry mountains and making his way to Glencar, and eventually taking refuge with the chief of the McClancys at Rossclogher castle, on an island in Lough Melvin, on the borders of Connacht and Ulster (**77, 99**).

On hearing of the approach of Fitzwilliam, the Lord Deputy, who was scouring the countryside for Armada survivors, MacClancy fled to the hills, leaving Cuellar and a handful of his compatriots to defend Rossclogher castle. This they did successfully, so that when MacClancy returned from hiding, he wished the heroic Spaniards to become his guard. However, Cuellar and four others slipped away, and made their way across Ulster to O'Cahan's country in north Derry, and thence to the vicinity of Dunluce castle. There they were succoured by Sorley Boy MacDonnell, who eventually arranged for them to sail across to Scotland. In that neutral land there was but cold comfort: 'It was said that the King of Scotland protected all the Spaniards who reached his kingdom, clothed them, and gave them passages to Spain; but all was the reverse, for he did no good to anyone, nor did he bestow one dollar in charity.' For six months Cuellar and his compatriots eked out an exile's life in Scotland, but at length he was befriended by some Catholic gentlemen, who contacted Parma in the Netherlands, and arranged for a Scottish vessel to take them there. On 4 October 1589 Cuellar finally arrived in Antwerp, having suffered shipwreck off Dunkirk, and narrowly avoiding capture by the Dutch (**77**).

There was a marked contrast between the ruthless treatment accorded to the Spanish survivors in Munster and Connacht, and the help they received from men like MacSweeny Banagh and O'Donnell in western Ulster. This arose because the latter was an area in which the Queen's writ could be ignored, whereas Munster and Connacht had been largely subdued and brought under English law. Fitzwilliam, who in mid-September had assured Burghley that, 'God hath fought by shipwrecks, savages and famine for Her Majesty against these proud Spaniards', was sufficiently concerned about the dangers of collusion between the northern chieftains and groups of Spanish survivors to undertake a journey to the north-west. He was at Athlone on 10 November and there began his northward march, 'wherein, if either the deepness of winter, which yieldeth short days and long nights, foul ways, great waters, many stormy showers, want of horsemeat, hazard of spoiling . . . besides the report that there were not above one hundred . . . of the ragged Spaniards would have persuaded me to stay, I should not have gone forwards' (**18, 6**). The Lord Deputy marched to Sligo, and on his way to Ballyshannon visited Streedagh strand. The corpses, of whom there had been about 1,200, had by this time been buried, but the wreckage remained: 'I rode along that strand near two mile,' wrote Fitzwilliam to the Privy Council, '[where] there lay as great store of the timber of wrecked ships . . . more than would have built five of the greatest ships that ever I saw, besides mights good boats, cables, and other cordage answerable thereunto' (**18**). From Streedagh, Fitzwilliam turned inland to attack Rossclogher castle, which was defended, as we have seen, by Captain Cuellar and his compatriots. Frustrated by their stout defence, the Lord Deputy continued his progress into Tyrconnell, where he parleyed with O'Donnell and other chiefs, exacting from them fair words and promises of payment of arrears of tribute.

As for MacClancy of Rossclogher he was eventually cornered by Sir Richard Bingham in April 1590. He 'ran for a lough which was near and tried to save himself by swimming, but a shot broke his arm, and a gallowglass brought him ashore. . . . He was the most barbarous creature in Ireland, and had always 100 knaves about him. . . . He was O'Rourke's right hand' (**18**). O'Rourke, the lord of Leitrim, who had also aided some of the Spanish survivors, fled to Scotland but was arrested there and sent to London, where he was executed for high treason.

These cases provided a grim indication that the government was now determined to extend its sway over western Ulster. Elizabeth and her ministers could not permit Ireland to be an Achilles heel in the war with Spain, as the Dutch Republic had proved to be for Philip II.

9 The War in Ulster, 1592-98

> Now sways it this way, like a mighty sea
> Forc'd by the tide to combat with the wind;
> Now sways it that way, like the self-same sea
> Forc'd to retire by fury of the wind:
> Sometime the flood prevails, and then the wind;
> Now one the better, then another best;
> Both tugging to be victors, breast to breast,
> Yet neither conqueror nor conquered:
> So is the equal poise of this fell war.

> W. SHAKESPEARE, *King Henry the Sixth*, Part Three, II, v.

RISE OF HUGH O'NEILL

After the murder of Shane O'Neill in 1567 and the failure of the colonising endeavours of Sir Thomas Smith and the Earl of Essex, the Dublin government followed a policy of conciliation in Ulster. It was a continuation of the policy of 'surrender and re-grant', mixed with the prudent principle of balancing one chief against the other. For instance, Hugh O'Neill, the second son of Matthew, Baron of Dungannon, and grandson of Con Bacach O'Neill, was regarded as a valuable counterweight to old Turlough Luineach O'Neill and to Shane O'Neill's progeny, the MacShanes. Hugh was born about 1545, and had been brought to England to be educated as a royal ward in 1562. There he was attached to the household of the Earl of Leicester and 'trooped in the streets of London with sufficient equipage and orderly respect' (**18, 4**). Hugh returned to Ireland in 1568, a year after the murder of his kinsman Shane O'Neill, and was put in possession of lands in Irish Oriel (Armagh) by the Lord Deputy, Sir Henry Sidney. In 1574 he helped Essex against Sir Brian McPhelim O'Neill of Clandeboy, but after the failure of the 'Enterprise of Ulster' in 1575, began to think of reaching some kind of agreement with old Turlough. So began his Janus-like attitude if balancing loyalty to the Crown against his own reasonable ambitions in Ulster. Indeed it was rumoured in 1584 that Hugh O'Neill had been elected as Turlough's tanist. This did not prevent him from accompanying Perrot on his expedition to north Antrim. O'Neill was rewarded for this service by elevation to the peerage as

Earl of Tyrone, and as such sat in the third parliament of Elizabeth's reign in 1585–6 (**26, 108**). Simultaneously he was consolidating his position in Ulster so that 'all men of rank within the province are become his men, receive his wages, and promise him service according to the usual manner of that country'.

Hugh O'Neill's first wife was a daughter of O'Neill of Clandeboy, and his second wife one of the O'Donnells. Both of these marriages were clearly explicable in purely 'dynastic' terms, but his third marriage was not. Hugh formed an attachment for Mabel Bagenal, daughter of Sir Nicholas Bagenal of Newry, who represented the intrusive English interest which threatened any attempt to revive the O'Neill supremacy in Ulster. Hugh O'Neill seems to have been infatuated and eloped with the young lady from her sister's house in co. Meath, whither she had been sent so that she might see less of him. They were married by the Bishop of Meath, who perhaps was moved by O'Neill's submission that it 'would bring civility into my house and among the country people'. Marshal Bagenal was furious, and, as he had predicted, the match proved to be unhappy, for it lasted only a few years. Nevertheless, it illustrated clearly the twofold desire of O'Neill to be a peer among the Anglo-Irish as well as embodying the princely independence of the great O'Neills. Torn between two civilisations, O'Neill could hardly fail to be accused of duplicity (**57, 61, 6,** chs. xliv, xlv).

CAMPAIGNS ON THE ULSTER BORDERS

A younger and more dynamic leader reappeared on the scene in Ulster with the dramatic escape of Red Hugh O'Donnell from Dublin castle in December 1591 (**17,** pp. 177–80). Red Hugh, the son of Hugh O'Donnell and Finola MacDonnell, was only fifteen when Perrot had taken him, under false pretences, from Rathmullen to Dublin, there to be imprisoned with other noble hostages [**doc. 13**]. On his return he drove the English troops out of the castle and abbey in Donegal, and was shortly afterwards inaugurated as chief of the O'Donnells in his father's room. Next year (1593) on the resignation of Turlough Luineach O'Neill, Hugh O'Neill was at last elected to the proud title 'The O'Neill'. The assumption of these emotive titles by the two allies indicated clearly that the Gaelic order in Ulster was prepared to resist further encroachment of English law.

O'Donnell brought over 3,000 Scottish mercenaries and with these troops went to the aid of Hugh Maguire, the 'Lion of the Erne'. The latter was in the front line after the downfall of MacClancy and O'Rourke of Leitrim. In 1592 there was fighting near Enniskillen, the island controlling the crossing of the river between upper and lower Lough Erne. Here Maguire had employed Scottish masons in the 1580s to build a Water-gate to defend the fifteenth-century stone castle, of which the poet Tadhg Dall O'Higgin wrote:

> Alas for him who looks upon Enniskillen, with its glistening bays and melodious falls; it is perilous for us, since one cannot forsake it, to look upon the fair castle with its shining sward. . . .
> This was the saying of each man regarding the splendid dwelling of the Lion of the Erne—no man in Banbha ever saw a habitation to equal it (**17**, pp. 335-7).

This majestic castle was taken by an English force, but was soon after recaptured by Hugh Maguire and Hugh Roe O'Donnell who were helped at one remove by Tyrone, through his brother Cormac MacBaron O'Neill. In May 1593 Maguire raided Sligo and Roscommon, and Bagenal was ordered to take the field against him, aided by Tyrone. They routed Maguire near the ford of the Erne at Belleek, with a loss of a quarter of his force. In the engagement Tyrone was wounded, and still more hurt by Bagenal's slighting references to him in his despatches. Following this victory Enniskillen castle was again taken by an English force in February 1594, but the victors were themselves besieged by Maguire and O'Donnell. In June 1594 the two latter successfully ambushed an English relief force at a ford over the river Arney in south Fermanagh. 'Many steeds, weapons, and other spoils were left behind in that place, besides the steeds and horses that were loaded with provisions on their way to Enniskillen. . . . The name of the ford . . . was changed to the . . . Ford of the Biscuits from the number of biscuits and small cakes left there to the victors on that day (**74, 100**).

Tyrone, still playing his double game, and still reluctant to launch himself on the path of open treason and rebellion, made his way to Dublin to pay his respects to Lord Russell, Fitzwilliam's successor as Lord Deputy. The latter accepted his submission, and shortly afterwards set out to relieve the starving garrison of Enniskillen castle. He arrived just in time on 30 August 1594 to find them eating rats and dogs. Tyrone did nothing to stop Russell's march. He was biding his time, resolved not to waste his carefully husbanded forces on chance skirmishes. He had been permitted by the Queen to have a force of 600 men, trained by six English captains. As soon as these men had completed their training, they were replaced with raw recruits, so that the approved regiment became a training cadre for what was virtually a small army. Gallowglasses were out of date by this time, for they were better adapted to swords and battleaxes than to firearms, and the device of the 'rising out' or hosting of the free-men, the 'natural people of Ulster, who are not chargeable unto him, but such as yield him revenue', was no longer a satisfactory method of waging war. The bulk of Tyrone's army consisted of mercenaries (called bonaghts) who were either Scottish gallowglasses or native Irish troops. Each year in the spring recruits were called for, and rates of pay and terms of service announced. The bonaghts were grouped in companies of 100, each under a constable or captain. By 1601 they were being paid threepence a day, with a bounty of four shillings twice a year, exclusive of their keep. In 1594 no fewer than 2000 bonaghts were enrolled and billeted, and as the war developed the numbers doubled and trebled, fed by the herds of cattle and extensive fields of corn in Tyrone, munitioned from the magazines hidden on crannogs in the lakes beyond the military frontier of the Blackwater (**98**).

Under their English and Spanish officers Tyrone's men were 'infinitely belaboured with training in all parts of Ulster', so that by 1595 his troops were 'far different from that which it was their wont to be, their numbers greater, and munitions more plenty with them'. Arms were imported from Scotland, through the agency principally of Glasgow merchants, from Danzig, from Spain, and smuggled from English seaports. The 4,000 men armed with guns in 1595 used calivers of 12 lb having a range of 150 yards, or muskets of 20 lb, with a range of 100 yards. Both these weapons fired balls of lead, some of it perhaps stripped from the roof of Dungannon castle. The musket-eers themselves had originated as kerne, or light native infantry, who had thus given up their sword or darts for more powerful weapons, just as, under Tyrone, the gallowglass had abandoned his two-handed axe for trailing a pike. Altogether Tyrone, on the eve of open rebellion, had some 1,000 pikemen, 4,000 musketeers, and 1,000 cavalry with which to meet the total of 1,100 troops at the Lord Deputy's disposal outside the province of Munster (100), [**doc. 22**]. Reinforcements were urgently required and 1,600 troops were shipped to Ireland from Brittany under Sir Henry Norris. A further 1,000 recruits of very mixed military value were raised in England and Sir John Norris was appointed to take command in Ulster. A third brother, Sir Thomas Norris was seconded to carry out the duties of the Lord President in Munster. All three Norris brothers were destined to die in the Irish campaigns (**74**).

In May 1595 Sir John Norris arrived at Waterford with his troops. It was a black period for English interests for in that same month Enniskillen was recaptured and Tyrone followed this up by besieging Monaghan castle. Sir Henry Bagenal marched from Newry with 1,500 men and succeeded in relieving it. On the return march Tyrone attacked Bagenal's force at Clontibret, his musketeers playing an important role in providing galling fire from the flanks. Bagenal lost 31 killed and 109 wounded, but was able to bring the remainder of his badly mauled force back to Newry (**79, 101**).

Meanwhile Sligo had fallen to Hugh Roe O'Donnell, with the result that the south-western approaches to Ulster were secured for the Gaelic cause. By now the cards were on the table and Tyrone was proclaimed a traitor on 30 June 1595.

THE YELLOW FORD, 1598

One result of the skirmish at Clontibret was that a truce was arranged in October 1595 to last until January 1596, which was subsequently extended until the opening of the campaigning season on 1 May. Meanwhile Monaghan castle fell to the MacMahons, and Sir Richard Bingham's attempt to recapture Sligo from the O'Donnells ended in failure. In short, the position was a stalemate. Tyrone tried to improve his position by fresh negotiations with Spain, carried out through Don Alonso de Cobos, who had arrived in Killybegs harbour, and a tortuous game of playing off the English and Spanish began [**doc. 18**], (**84, 85**). There was a curious repetition on a smaller scale in 1596-97 of the pattern of events in 1587-88, for Cadiz was attacked in 1596 and an Armada sailed on 14 October 1597 from Vigo and Lisbon, only to be dispersed by the autumnal gales. This effectively dashed Tyrone's hopes of receiving any effective aid from that quarter—aid without which in the long run he could not hope to sustain his rebellion.

The stalemate continued during 1597 during the brief Deputyship

of Lord Thomas Brough (May–October). A threefold attack on
Ulster was planned: first, the Lord Deputy was to march to the
Blackwater, and thence through Tyrone's and Maguire's territory
to Ballyshannon on the Erne; second, Conyers Clifford, the new
President of Connacht, who had already recaptured Sligo, was to
join Brough at Ballyshannon; third, Barnewall was to march from
Mullingar in Westmeath to the Erne. The joint forces would then
attack O'Neill and O'Donnell in strength, and force the war to its
climax. Each prong, however, of this threefold attack was repulsed.
Brough was defeated near Benburb on the Blackwater by O'Neill;
Clifford was thrown back by O'Donnell's men; Barnewall was
ambushed at Tyrrell's Pass. Nor surprisingly, another truce was
arranged in December 1597 to last until May 1598.

By July 1598 the garrison of the small fort at Portmore on the
Blackwater, which had been relieved by Brough, was again in
desperate straits. Bagenal marched from Newry to relieve it, for by
this time the garrison was living on horsemeat. Bagenal's army
consisted of nearly 4,000 infantry and some 320 cavalry, all well
equipped. By mid-August they had reached Armagh, but on con-
tinuing their march on 14–15 August they were engaged by Tyrone
and O'Donnell at the Yellow Ford on the river Callan. Tyrone's
kerne were armed with muskets, and taking every advantage of cover
and mobility, provided sharp fire on the flanks of Bagenal's force.
The latter had divided his men into six regiments, but by the time of
the hottest engagement at the Yellow Ford, the force had become
too dispersed for effective support to be given to the leading regiment,
which was forced to retreat from the galling fire and was largely
cut to pieces by cavalry. Dashing forward to prevent a rout, Bagenal
was shot dead, and his regiment was decimated by well-directed
musket fire and well-timed cavalry charges. Eventually, under
Sir Thomas Wingfield, a rout was prevented and a retreat was
carried out, some 1,500 of Bagenal's original force reaching Armagh
(**73, 75, 79**), [**doc. 23**].

The battle of the Yellow Ford was a decisive victory. It indicated
the value of Tyrone's insistence on proper training, his careful
arming of his men, and his combination of the mobility of the older
Irish pattern of battle, with a disciplined control of his troops.
The fort on the Blackwater surrendered on generous terms, Armagh
was evacuated, and the proposed English landing at Derry was
abandoned. Such were the immediate military results of this remark-

able Irish victory. However, although Tyrone now appeared to be at the apex of his rebellion, he had merely won a battle. The more solid fruits of victory in his eventual aims continued to elude him. Paradoxically, the defeat of the Yellow Ford, made Tyrone's downfall certain, as the Queen was so incensed that no matter what the cost, she was determined to finish the war and complete the pacification of Ireland.

10 The End of the Gaelic Order

> Cry, havoc, kings! back to the stained field,
> You equal potentates, fiery kindled spirits!
> Then let confusion of one part confirm
> The other's peace; till then blows, blood, and death!

W. SHAKESPEARE, *King John*, II. i.

THE ESSEX EPISODE

Philip II of Spain died in 1598, the year of O'Neill's victory at the Yellow Ford. He died at the moment when Spain had begun to feel the strain of prolonged war on the European scale. The attempt to crush the rebellious Dutch, the intervention in the civil war in France, the costly failure of the Armadas of 1588 and 1596, all proved to be such a strain on Spanish finance and administration that she embarked on a policy of disengagement under Philip III. This implied, among other moves, attempting to extract better peace terms from Elizabeth's government by creating a diversion in Ireland. From the Spanish point of view Ireland was but a pawn in a game, in which the Netherlands, England, France, Savoy and the Indies were more important pieces. Hugh O'Neill's hopes of decisive Spanish help after the victory of the Yellow Ford were therefore unlikely to be realised in the current mood of Spanish policy (**84, 85**).

In 1599 the Queen's favourite, Robert Devereux, 2nd Earl of Essex was appointed as Lord Lieutenant of Ireland, and provided with an army of some 16,000 infantry and 1300 cavalry—the largest force which had so far been raised for service in Ireland. He arrived in Dublin on 15 April 1599, and unwisely allowed himself to be sidetracked into dealing with the endemic problems of King's and Queen's counties, where the O'Mores and O'Connors continued their opposition to the policy of confiscation and plantation. Essex suffered a defeat near Maryborough, and then, turning to deal with the O'Byrnes and O'Tooles in the Wicklow mountains, suffered another reverse in the wild and rocky defile of Glenmalure. Disease, desertion and defeat played such havoc with his troops that by July he only had 4,000 out of his original paper strength of 17,300 fit for service. To add to Essex's discomfiture Sir Conyers Clifford, the

governor of Connacht, was defeated in the Curlew mountains in
Roscommon by O'Donnell and O'Rourke, and his headless body
buried on an island in Lough Key (**6, 74**).

Essex was left with no resource but to follow the worn pattern of
parleying with Tyrone, which he did at the ford of Annaclint, on
the border of Monaghan and Louth. This was a tactical victory for
O'Neill, who was always anxious to play for time, but it was disastrous for Essex. He left Ireland on 24 September 1599, returned to
London, raised a madcap rebellion, and was beheaded early in 1600
(**103, 71**).

MOUNTJOY IN COMMAND

Elizabeth now had to look for a capable general who could save the
situation in Ireland and deal effectively with Tyrone. She selected
Charles Blount, Lord Mountjoy. At length the hour and the man
were matched. Charles Brooke Blount, 8th Lord Mountjoy, born in
1563, was a typical Elizabethan younger son of an ancient family
which had become impoverished. His pathway to fortune opened up,
not in Oxford or the Inner Temple, but at court, where he quickly
found favour with Elizabeth, even ousting Sir Walter Raleigh by
1586. His early rivalry with Essex soon changed into a friendly
alliance, and he saw service under Sir John Norris in the Netherlands
in 1585. He was present at the skirmish at Zutphen in 1586, and was
knighted by Leicester in 1587. In 1588 Mountjoy commanded the
Lion during the passage of the Spanish Armada up the English
Channel, and was subsequently rewarded by being appointed one
of the Queen's Gentlemen Pensioners—a sinecure which resolved
his personal financial worries, and in 1593 he became governor of
Portsmouth, in which place he applied himself to the study of
fortification and the use of sea power in assisting military operations.
This experience was to bear fruit in Ireland, where Mountjoy's
campaigns during his brief Lord Deputyship afforded one of the
earliest examples in modern history of the coordination of the land
and sea arms.

Mountjoy landed at Howth near Dublin on 26 February 1600.
Within a few days he had been sworn in and had taken a firm grip
of the administrative and military machine. His was a temperament
'which the Irish disliked, almost feared. He spoke little and when

87

he did his judgment was decisive; he promised less, but once having pledged his word he stood to it through thick and thin' (**81, 82**). A tall man with a balding head, smoking tobacco as a specific against the damp and chills of Ireland, he had something of the puritan about him. Retiring and grave in outlook, unlike the extrovert Essex, he read widely in the Fathers and Schoolmen, and, unlike the colourful Perrot, 'never used swearing, but rather hated it . . . he was slow to anger, but once provoked spake home' (**17,** pp. 199–202). Mountjoy soon restored the shattered morale of the troops by his personal courage in the forefront of battle, and by his reliance on capable subordinates [**doc. 24**]. Of these two were outstanding: Sir George Carew in Munster, and Sir Arthur Chichester in Ulster. Both were Devonians, Carew being a cousin of the Sir Peter Carew whose land-grabbing had triggered off the first Desmond rebellion, and Chichester being a brother of the Sir John Chichester who had taken Shane's castle from the O'Neills of Clandeboy and had been killed in a skirmish with Sorley Boy MacDonnell and the Antrim Scots in 1597 (**110, 59**).

Sir George Carew was appointed president of Munster. That province had been devastated by a widespread rising against the planters in 1598. This had been partly caused by discontents accumulating over the previous decade, and partly stimulated by O'Neill's success at the battle of the Yellow Ford, and the subsequent incursion of some of his troops into Munster. In October 1598 'the Munster rebellion broke out like a lightning, for in one month's space almost all the Irish were in rebellious arms'. The Munster undertakers themselves had in many cases alienated their lands to the native Irish, many were habitual absentees, those who were resident had neglected to build castles or fortified dwellings, and had not brought over a sufficient number of English tenants, indeed they 'brought no more English than their own families, and all entertained Irish servants and tenants, which were now the first to betray them'. Now in October 1598 much of the plantation was undone: 'These combinations and revolts have effected many execrable murders and cruelties upon the English, as well in the county of Limerick, as in the counties of Cork and Kerry, and else-where; . . . by view whereof the English might the more bitterly lament the misery of their countrymen, and fear the like to befall to themselves' (**6,** ch. xlvii; **17,** pp. 211–12).

In January 1600 Tyrone marched south through Cavan, Westmeath and Tipperary. There he endeavoured to build up a confederacy among the Munster rebels under his leadership, cemented together by the spirit of the Counter-Reformation and buoyed up by hopes of Spanish aid. However, his ally and son-in-law, Hugh Maguire, was killed in a skirmish near Cork, and he determined to return to Ulster, where his real strength lay, leaving behind Florence MacCarthy as the main leader of rebellion in the South (**4**). Sir George Carew had on paper some 3000 infantry (1740 in effect) to deal with an estimated 7000 rebels in arms. Yet by playing off one man against another, by forcing the O'Connor mercenaries to return to Connacht, by the skilful use of artillery to enforce the surrender of such vital castles as Glin, Carrickafoyele, Lixnaw and Tralee, and by defeating James Fitzthomas, the would-be Earl of Desmond, near Kilmallock, Carew succeeded in pacifying the province of Munster by the end of 1600, and was even able to send a force of 1000 to serve in Connacht (**20**).

The defeat of Tyrone and the reduction of Ulster were to Mountjoy always the prime considerations, and all his energies were devoted to those ends. Accordingly in May 1600 troops were sent by sea to Carrickfergus from Dublin under the command of Sir Henry Docwra. While they waited at Carrickfergus, Mountjoy assembled a force of some 3,500 (out of the total available to him in Ireland of 1,200 cavalry and 14,000 infantry) at Drogheda. Mountjoy marched his army to Dundalk and thence northward towards Newry through 'a broaken cawsey besette on both sydes with bogges, where the Irish might skyppe but the English could not goe; and on the two endes . . . it was naturally fenced with short and shrubbed wood' (**80, 74**). This was the Moyry pass, part of the easternmost defences of O'Neill's territories known as 'Tyrone's Ditches', and a strategic route linking the Pale to English bases in Down and Antrim. Mountjoy was thus threatening Tyrone's south-eastern flank. He reacted by retreating to the line of the river Blackwater, and while he was so engaged Docwra's force landed on the Foyle, establishing forts at Culmore and at Derry. So, by 16 May Mountjoy and Docwra had achieved their first objective: the establishment of a base in the north-west. Yet, Mountjoy was left under no illusions about the difficulty of bringing down such an experienced and wily opponent as Tyrone. This was demonstrated on 17 May when the force under the Earl of Southampton and Sir Oliver Lambert, escorted by 500 of Mountjoy's men, was attacked by Tyrone's men in the Moyry pass,

89

and almost prevented from reaching Newry. Indeed, Mountjoy himself judged it prudent to return to Dublin by way of Carlingford rather than attempt the pass back to Dundalk and the Pale.

Mountjoy had now determined upon a winter campaign against Tyrone and so he wished to secure the Pale by a swift and ruthless foray against the perennial rebels in King's and Queen's counties. In a month, from 25 July until 26 August, Mountjoy conducted a flying campaign in the Midlands, seizing cattle, destroying crops, and finally killing Owny O'More of Leix. Fynes Moryson, who was Mountjoy's secretary, observed the reluctance of the common soldiers to cut down the rebel's corn, and was astonished to find 'that by so barbarous inhabitants, the ground should be so manured, the fields so orderly fenced, the towns so frequently inhabited, and the highways and paths so well beaten, as the Lord Deputy here found them' (**28**).

In September 1600 Mountjoy began his winter campaign and encamped north of Dundalk at Faughart, historic scene of the defeat of Edward Bruce in 1318. He faced the Moyry pass once more, which had meantime been freshly fortified by Tyrone who had 'made in the wood and highway divers trenches and barricades in the manner of little sconces with great hedges on the top' (**80**) The rainy weather prevented any attack on the Moyry fortification until 2 October. For two days a dour and bitter struggle raged, which 'on the minute scale of Irish warfare, was Mountjoy's Somme, with a like calamitious effect upon the side which stood upon the defensive (**74**). Mountjoy drove his opponents out of their trenches, but at a cost of some fifty killed and 200 wounded. Both sides withdrew Mountjoy to Newry and Tyrone to Armagh. Later, Mountjoy returned to the Moyry and levelled the entrenchments and cleared away the abbatis of trees and brushwood (**79**). Finally, he abandoned the idea of advancing to Armagh and contented himself with consolidating his victory by building a campaign fort halfway between Newry and Armagh, which was named Mount Norris in honour of Mountjoy's former commander Sir John Norris. This fort was thrown up by the troops in four days on the site of an old ring-fort or rath (**80**).

Tough though this winter campaigning was it showed clearly th extraordinary improvements in morale and discipline on both side (**98, 102**). Tyrone's men even tried to repeat the success of th Yellow Ford by ambushing Mountjoy's army as it marched pas

Narrow Water on the road to Carlingford. However, Mountjoy was a better general than Bagenal and the spirit of his troops was such that Tyrone was beaten off, leaving Mountjoy with the strategic gains of the campaign of 1600, namely the forts at Culmore, Derry and Mount Norris, firmly in his hands.

Mountjoy, however, true to his intention, continued to harry his opponents right through the depth of winter [**doc. 24**]. He attacked the O'Byrnes and the O'Tooles in Wicklow, and harried O'Neill's ally Richard Tyrrell in Meath and Westmeath. This winter campaign was very effective, for such minor chieftains as Turlough O'Neill, O'Hanlon of Armagh, O'Kane of Derry, the lesser O'Neills of the Fews in Armagh, the lords of Farney in Monaghan and of Brefni (Cavan) expressed their willingness to submit to him (**81**). Indeed the outlook for 1601 was on the whole encouraging. Such rebels as there were in Connacht could easily be suppressed by troops sent from the key posts of Athlone and Boyle, Docwra had gained the alliance of Niall Garve O'Donnell (**96**), and, thanks to the O'Dohertys, was able to use the vast peninsula of Inishowen as his granary and supply base, while Chichester had already begun to build up a naval task force for service on Lough Neagh. There he had a decked barque of 30 tons, vessels of 14 tons, two of 10 tons and three smaller boats. With these he raided the western shores of Lough Neagh:

> We have burnt and destroyed along the Lough, even within four miles of Dungannon, from whence we returned hither yesterday; in which journeys we have killed above one hundred people of all sorts, besides such as were burnt, how many I know not. We spare none of what quality or sex soever, and it hath bred much terror in the people, who heard not a drum nor saw not a fire there of a long time.

Tyrone marvelled at these naval raids, and built a chain of field works at Clonoe, Ballinderry and Toome, which proved effective in checking Chichester's raids. Chichester's flotilla also raided the O'Neill lands of Killultagh on the eastern shores of Lough Neagh, making 'spoil of such corn, cattle and people as we met with'. Nonetheless, Chichester's main object was to attack Dungannon, for which he had 'sufficient store of boats, men, victuals, munition and tools at Massereene to be transported over the lough ...' (**18, 74, 110**).

In May (1601) Mountjoy set out once more for the north. This year he decided to maintain his grip on the Moyry pass by building a fort on the site of the meeting place of Shane O'Neill and the English in 1561. A Dutch engineer, 'his name is said to be Leuni Rose or such a like man', was employed to supervise the erection of a square, three-storied castle fitted with musketry loopholes, situated within a walled rectangular enclosure. Armagh was garrisoned, the citadel inevitably being the partially damaged cathedral, and in July Mountjoy marched thence to the Blackwater. The river was crossed and a new fort erected at Portmore (Blackwatertown). Essex had been the first to build a fort near Portmore in 1575, but this had been attacked and subsequently destroyed by Hugh O'Neill in 1595. Lord Burgh built a second fort at Portmore, consisting of an earthwork with a rampart and ditch in 1597, and now Mountjoy's men threw up their campaign earthwork on the southern bank on the site of a windmill at the Mullin. This was in plan a closed lunette with bastions containing some English-style houses for the troops and providing a defended crossing of the river into the O'Neill territories (**80**). To crown this achievement Mountjoy brought Tyrone to action at Benburb a few miles away and defeated him.

THE SIEGE OF KINSALE

Throughout 1601 Mountjoy and Carew had been in expectation of a Spanish landing in Ireland. This meant that neither Mountjoy nor Docwra, whose ally Niall Garve O'Donnell had successfully withstood a siege in Donegal Abbey, could bring matters to a conclusion in Ulster, without bearing in mind the possibility of a Spanish landing in Munster or Connacht. On 19 September Mountjoy was at Kilkenny conferring with the Earl of Ormond and Sir George Carew, and next day news came that a Spanish fleet had been sighted off the Old Head of Kinsale.

In January 1601 the Treaty of Lyons between France and Savoy relieved Spain of the necessity of helping the Savoyards. Consequently a force of some 6000 infantry was set aside for an expedition to Ireland, and eight months later was ready to set sail. By that time there were only 4,432 effectives under the command of Don Juan del Aguila, a commander known to and approved by both Hugh O'Neill and Red Hugh O'Donnell (**104**). The two Ulster leaders naturally wanted the Spanish expedition to make for a port or beach on the west coast, just as in 1796 the United Irishmen wanted the French to land in Ulster, rather than Bantry Bay in west Cork. But in 1601, as in 1796, the weather played its part in rearranging plans for a suitable landfall. Don Pedro de Zubiaur with 650 men in nine vessels was driven back by an autumn gale, and the decision about the landfall was left to del Aguila. It was indeed probable that the fleet had originally hoped to reach Galway, but stormy weather drove them back towards Munster, and it was agreed by del Aguila and his captains that the fleet should set course for a port on the south coast. This decision was reinforced shortly afterwards by a fierce gale which forced nine vessels with 650 men under Don Pedro de Zubiaur to make their way back to Spain. So it was with a battered and reduced force of some 4,800 men that Aguila finally landed at Kinsale on 2 October 1601 to begin his memorable 100 days in Ireland (**119, 105, 107, 120**). Kinsale, like Dingle and Dungarvan, was a port of secondary importance. A walled town of some 200 houses it lay on a curve of the Bandon river near its mouth, the approaches upstream from the sea being protected by two forts: Ringcurran and Castle Park (map 5). The small garrison offered no resistance to the Spaniards; 'the Sovereign with his white rod in his hands, going to billet, and cease them in several houses, more ready than if they had been the Queen's forces' (**20**).

Mountjoy, knowing that Carew had laid in plentiful supplies of munition and forage against the possibility of a Spanish landing, wasted little time in collecting his troops at Cork. By 17 October he encamped in Knockrobin hill overlooking Kinsale from the north. Between this camp and the walls of Kinsale ran an inlet of the sea called Oysterhaven, which lay just beyond cannon shot from the town. This creek served as a sheltered landing place for Mountjoy's siege guns and heavy supplies, and enabled him to establish a regular siege camp to the north, from whose earthworks and gabions his guns began to play upon the Spaniards early in November. All this was accomplished in the face of spirited Spanish counterattacks. Mountjoy's first task was to silence the outlying Spanish forts at Ringcurran and Castle Park. Ringcurran lay on the eastern bank of the Bandon river, and Mountjoy's guns commenced bombardment on 30 October, and early on 1 November the fort surrendered and the captured Spanish garrison sent as prisoners to Cork—an interesting contrast to the fate of the defenders of Smerwick (**20, 81**).

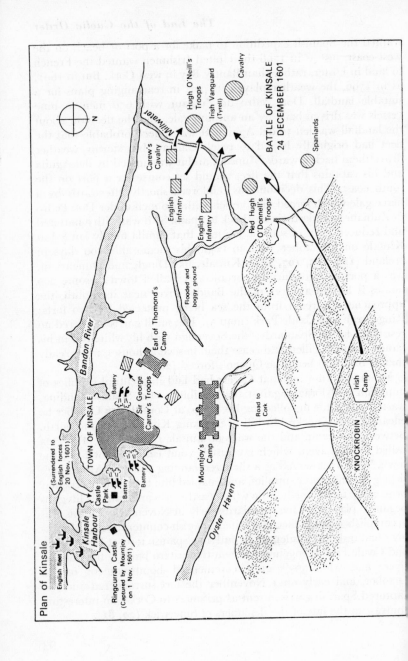

Plan of Kinsale

BATTLE OF KINSALE 24 DECEMBER 1601

N

Bandon River

Millwater

Hugh O'Neill's Troops

Irish Vanguard (Tyrell)

Cavalry

Carew's Cavalry

English Infantry

English Infantry

Spaniards

Red Hugh O'Donnell's Troops

Flooded and boggy ground

Earl of Thomond's Camp

Sir George Carew's Troops

Battery

Battery

TOWN OF KINSALE

Castle Park

Battery

Kinsale Harbour

English fleet

(Surrendered to English forces 20 Nov. 1601)

Ringcurran Castle (Captured by Mountjoy on 1 Nov. 1601)

Mountjoy's Camp

Road to Cork

Oyster Haven

KNOCKROBIN

Irish Camp

During November Mountjoy was under considerable pressure to release his hold on Kinsale. The northern earls were slowly marching south, raiding and devastating as they marched; the people of the Pale complained of their lack of protection; the Spaniards were well entrenched and were fighting tenaciously, repulsing the first attacks on Castle Park successfully (**20, 107**). Yet, Mountjoy saw that by refusing to lift the ever-tightening siege, he would remain in control of the military situation and bring matters to a conclusion at Kinsale, so forcing Tyrone and O'Donnell to give battle on ground of his choosing. During November the siege became tighter; Castle Park finally fell on 20 November, a Spanish sortie was repulsed, and the final stage began. Mountjoy's guns began to bombard the town: 'To break their houses that they might find no safety in them and thereby to be exposed to the like incommodity of wind, cold and rain as we felt in the camp' (**17**). The weather that season had been unusually harsh and inclement; small wonder that both Mountjoy and Carew looked forward to a happy reunion when their service ended in 'the land of good meat and clean linen' (**19**).

By the beginning of December the English trenches had been extended to the west side of the town, the side from which relief might be expected to come from the approaching Irish. The Spaniards replied with a ferocious sally against the English works, and were shortly afterwards heartened by the news that Admiral Zubiaur with ten ships had reached Castlehaven in west Cork. To crown all, Tyrone now arrived, joined O'Donnell, and appeared at the head of what looked like a numerous and powerful confederacy of the Munster lords. Mountjoy's troops were now themselves besieged from without, and their lines of landward communication with Cork threatened.

In this critical situation Mountjoy had only one real hope: that of forcing the Irish to fight a battle in the open field. In such a situation he was confident of victory, for the Irish strength lay in guerrilla warfare, and in any event the northern leaders were as divided in counsel as were Marsin and the Elector before the battle of Blenheim. O'Donnell had been the first to move south. He had raised the siege of Niall Garve O'Donnell's men in Donegal Abbey, assembled his forces near Sligo, marched through Roscommon, crossed the Shannon, and plundered his way through the Butler lands of Tipperary. Tyrone started his move southwards just when O'Donnell was crossing the Shannon. He moved slowly, as always playing for time and waiting on events. Early in December the two northern leaders joined forces with 8,000 men at their disposal. Del Aguila urged them to attack in conjunction with a Spanish sortie from Kinsale; Tyrone favoured the policy of encircling Mountjoy's forces, and weakening them by attrition and famine, while Red Hugh wished to accept the gage of battle. O'Donnell's view prevailed. The Irish forces now occupied Knockrobin hill to the north of Mountjoy's main camp. There they were in a strong defensive position, looking down on Oysterhaven and beyond to the siege lines. However, it was decided to mount the attack on the western side. This meant moving under cover of darkness across Mountjoy's flank, leaving the protection of the high ground, and maintaining proper formation in the flooded and boggy morasses which formed a natural protection for the English trenches to the west of the town. The result on 24 December 1601 was less of a battle than a rout. Tyrone's men were drawn back in order to regroup, but these orders were misunderstood, and Mountjoy's disciplined veterans and his admirable use of cavalry carried the day with astonishing ease. Both Mountjoy and del Aguila were surprised at the collapse of the Irish pack of cards. The lack of cohesion and of secrecy among the Irish (for their plans had been betrayed to the English by Brian Oge MacMahon), prevented del Aguila from mounting a coordinated sortie from Kinsale, and his job after the battle was quite simply to conclude affairs on the best terms he could. This he did on 2 January 1602 by articles which the Spanish were to quit Kinsale, Castlehaven, Baltimore and Berehaven, and were to be transported back to Spain. Kinsale may have completed the work of the Armada in the downfall of Spain, but it also paved the way for the general peace between England and Spain in 1604. So, from the viewpoint of Spanish diplomacy del Aguila had fulfilled a valuable function in creating such a diversion in Ireland as would make satisfactory peace negotiations more likely (**101, 120**).

Red Hugh O'Donnell sailed with Zubiaur to Spain to try to enlist further help, but died, it was said of poison, at Salamanca in 1602. Tyrone marched slowly back to Ulster, attacked as he went by those whose property had been plundered on the southern journey, while in Dunboy castle O'Sullivan Beare made a famous 'last stand' against Carew's forces. Mountjoy, the patient and victorious general, travelled slowly back to Dublin, too ill yet to realise the full extent of his achievement or to begin planning his final campaign. (**20, 29**).

FINAL HARVEST, 1602–03

The net was inexorably closing round Tyrone and the campaign of 1602 proved decisive. Chichester was the first to take action in early March with a raid across Lough Neagh with 140 men, who returned, having performed such service that it made 'Tyrone take care, and look behind him. . . . I have lately finished a vessel of 25 tons, which I hope to use for planting garrisons on the other side of the lough.' By May Mountjoy had recovered his health sufficiently to leave Dublin for Ulster, and on 10 June he was at Newry with an army of 4000 men. He marched to the Blackwater, and established a square entrenchment on the banks of the river several miles north of the fort of the Mullin. This new fort he called Charlemont, and here Captain Toby Caulfield was left in command of the garrison. Dungannon was taken, and a conference took place between Mountjoy, Chichester and Docwra. They decided that Docwra and Chichester would combine to harass Tyrone in his last stronghold in the woods and bogs of Glenconkein which lay north-west of Lough Neagh, and now was to the O'Neills what the Glen of Aherlow had been to the Desmonds. Mountjoy left a garrison in Dungannon, and 'spent some five days about Tullahogue, where the O'Neills were of old custom created, and . . . brake down the chair wherein the O'Neills were wont to be created, being of stone placed in the open field' (**80**). With this action, symbolic of the ending of the old Gaelic order, 'the axe was now at the root of the tree'. Mountjoy further consolidated his grip on the south-western shores of Lough Neagh by constructing a campaign fort near Tyrone's fortifications at Clonoe. In a few days the ramparts afforded some protection for 100 cavalry and 1000 infantry; later a 'fair castle of stone and brick, covered with slate and tile' was added, standing beside the old fort (**44, 80**).

During the sharp winter of 1602–3 famine and destitution did Mountjoy's work for him and the Earl of Tyrone came to Mellifont in March 1603, 'making his penitent submission to the Queen'. News of her death was deliberately withheld from him; when he was told he wept copiously: 'There needed no Edipus to find out the true cause of his tears, for no doubt, the most humble submission he made to the Queen he had so highly and proudly offended, much eclipsed the vainglory his actions might have carried, if he had held out till her death' (**17**).

Part Three

POSTSCRIPT

11 The Jacobean Settlement

> I had rather labour with my hands in the plantation of Ulster
> than dance or play in that of Virginia.
>
> SIR ARTHUR CHICHESTER

The surrender of Tyrone at Mellifont in March 1603 symbolised the defeat of Gaelic Ireland and was the ceremonial culmination of the long period of reconquest which had occupied Elizabeth's entire reign. With the accession of James I, the Crowns of the three Kingdoms of Scotland, England and Ireland were at last united. The kingdom of Ireland, established by Henry VIII in 1541, was now a reality. For the first time in history one government and one system of law prevailed over the entire country. The King's peace now covered the whole realm, a fact made plain to all by the judges on assize in areas which up to now had been shire ground on paper only. Sir Arthur Chichester, who succeeded Mountjoy as Lord Deputy, issued a proclamation of English law in 1605, and in the same year Sir John Davies, the Attorney General, gave judgment against the brehon law practices of tanistry and gavelkind [**docs. 14, 5**]. All were now subjects under Common Law, and the distinction between those who lived under the King's peace and those who had in the past been called 'the King's Irish enemies' ceased. So, too, the Gaelic chiefs lost their jurisdictions and their accustomed 'cuttings and spendings' [**doc. 2**].

For the Anglo-Irish 1603 also marked an important turning-point. Under the Tudors their control over the Irish parliament had been curtailed by Poynings' Law [**doc. 6**], and they had been replaced in the Dublin administration by officials who were English by birth. The fall of the house of Kildare in 1535 was as inevitable as the fate of the overmighty subjects in England, and was indicative of the steady growth in the power of the Crown. This process was accelerated under Elizabeth with the supersession of the palatine jurisdictions, the setting-up of the conciliar Presidencies in Munster and Connacht, and the crushing of the rebellious Geraldines of Desmond. In the parliaments of Elizabeth's reign the Anglo-Irish increasingly found themselves in the position of a 'country' party, in opposition to the 'court' party of new settlers and Tudor officials. The result was that, in the parliament summoned by Chichester in 1613–15, the Anglo-Irish found themselves outnumbered and politically sterilised by the influx of members for the newly created boroughs plus the 'new men' who had settled in Ireland under Elizabeth and James I (**108**).

The accession of James I also proved to be of significance in religious affairs. Now that the Kingdom had been reduced to 'civility' it was possible to give reality to the Elizabethan church settlement [**doc. 30**]. Under Elizabeth there had of necessity been a large measure of practical toleration; now, it was possible to insist on conformity, although this meant enforcing the law on a largely Catholic population. At first, particularly in the towns of Munster, it was thought that James I, the son of Mary, Queen of Scots, would deal gently with catholicism, and Mass was celebrated openly. Mountjoy and Chichester, however, soon ended these manifestations, although both men believed in toleration in practice. James I made his position clear at the Hampton Court Conference in 1604, and in the following year Chichester issued a proclamation against religious toleration in Ireland [**doc. 19**]. This decision was resented by those of the Anglo-Irish who were recusant, especially the lords of the Pale, and forced many of them into an uneasy alliance with the gentry of Gaelic stock, cemented by their common religion. The results were to be seen in the War of the Three Kingdoms, 1641–49, and the support given to the Jacobite cause in 1689–91. Further, the attempted enforcement of the Elizabethan church settlement led, step by step, to the dispossession of many Catholic landowners and to the persecuting and disabling Penal Code of the early eighteenth century.

After the scene at Mellifont, Hugh O'Neill and Rory O'Donnell travelled under Mountjoy's protection to London. There they renewed their submission to the Crown. James, following the now obsolete policy of 'surrender and re-grant', pardoned them and confirmed them in their earldoms of Tyrone and Tyrconnell. They returned to their diminished estates—for their former urraghts like O'Cahan of Derry had been granted their own territories—to find an altered world. They were surrounded by land-hungry adventurers and servitors (ex-servicemen) who hoped that their estates would be confiscated, as had happened to the Desmond lands in Munster. They had lost all the privileges they had had as Gaelic chiefs, and were enmeshed in the web of English law and local administration. Finally, in 1607, the two earls and their dependants sailed into exile from Rathmullan in Donegal [**doc. 31**]. The 'Flight of the Earls' was a dramatic admission of their inability to come to terms with the Jacobean 'brave new world'. It confirmed the fact that Kinsale had been a defeat for the forces of the Counter-Reformation, and emphasised a recognition that Ireland was firmly within the English sphere of influence, a situation strengthened by the union of the Crowns, and underscored by the peace with Spain in 1604. Tyrone now realised that his efforts to secure effective Spanish intervention on the Gaelic and Catholic side had been in vain [**doc. 18**]. His negotiations may be compared with the attempts made by the Stuarts in the seventeenth and eighteenth centuries to gain French help for a Jacobite restoration. In both cases European powers merely sought to stir up trouble for England in Ireland, just as, for example, the French helped the Hungarians to rebel against the Emperor. Neither the Spanish in the sixteenth century nor the French in the seventeenth or eighteenth centuries wished to intervene decisively in Irish affairs. This was an aspect of politics on which Hugh O'Neill had plenty of time to reflect before his death in Rome in 1616 (**85**).

The 'Flight of the Earls' heralded the downfall of the minor chieftains. Sir Cahir O'Doherty flew into rebellion in 1608, and forfeited the peninsula of Inishowen to Chichester. Niall Garve O'Donnell was accused of being party to O'Doherty's rebellion, and so both he and O'Cahan were imprisoned in the Tower, where they died some twenty years later. Their lands were confiscated and added to those already escheated to the Crown by the deaths of Hugh Maguire and Sir John O'Reilly before 1603, and the indictment of Tyrone and O'Donnell in 1607. Six Ulster counties now lay open for plantation, namely, Armagh, Cavan, Coleraine (now co. Derry), Donegal, Fermanagh and Tyrone (**12, 88**).

The plantation of Ulster was a continuation of that colonising process which had begun under Mary in the midland counties of Leix and Offaly. Under Elizabeth there had been the abortive schemes of Sir Thomas Smith and the Earl of Essex for the colonisation of Ulster, and the land-grabbing activities of men like Gilbert, Carew and Raleigh in Munster. Finally, after the attainder of the Desmonds, the plantation of Munster was attempted. It was a curious combination of state sponsorship and private exploitation, and did not make the same mark on Irish history as the later plantation of Ulster. That plantation was more carefully and thoroughly planned than the earlier experiments. The size of land grants was limited, stringent conditions were laid down about tenancies, and, in particular, the place to be occupied by 'meritorious natives', settlers were expected to build proper houses with defensible bawns (walled enclosures for cattle adjoining the dwelling), and the London Companies were persuaded to undertake the plantation of co. Derry (**86, 90**). It was a great enterprise and yet, so far as the escheated counties were concerned, it was only a qualified success. The British planters were fewer in number than had originally been hoped for, much land reverted to native Irish ownership, the towns and villages developed slowly, and, apart from timber and the salmon and eel fisheries, there were no mineral resources or cash crops like tobacco to attract immigrants, as there were in the American colonies [**doc. 32**]. The settlement of south Antrim and north Down by lowland Scottish settlers led by Sir James Hamilton and Sir Hugh Montgomery was a more successful venture and created a flourishing 'private enterprise' plantation in eastern Ulster (**87, 91**). In this, Moyses Hill, a Devonian, laid the foundations of the Downshire family fortune, Sir Fulke Conway introduced English and Welsh settlers to the formerly wild area of Killultagh, and Sir Arthur Chichester became lord of Belfast (which he valued at no more than £5 a year) and built for himself a magnificent Jacobean mansion at Joymount, Carrickfergus (**46, 89**).

Elizabethan Ireland had been rent by conflicts between the Tudor and Gaelic civilisations, between the Crown and the Anglo-Irish, and between Catholic and Protestant. By 1603 these issues had been decided, and by 1616, when both Sir Arthur Chichester and Hugh O'Neill were dead, Ireland had moved into modern times. As Sir John Davies summed up the solid achievements of Elizabeth's reign:

> Briefly, the clock of the civil government is now well set, and all the wheels thereof do move in order. The strings of this Irish harp which the civil magistrate doth finger are all in tune; . . . and make a good harmony in this Commonweal (**26**).

Part Four

DOCUMENTS

GAELIC SOCIETY

Tanistry

*To many of the Elizabethan English, Gaelic society in Ireland appeared
as strange as that of the North American Indians. Land belonged to the
freemen of the sept in each of the tuatha, rather than to the chief as his
estate. Succession to the chieftainship was not therefore through the
principle of primogeniture, but by the selection of a suitable adult male
from the kinship group during the lifetime of the ruling chief.*

The inheritance descendeth not to the son, but to the brother,
nephew or cousin-german eldest and most valiant: for the child
being oftentimes left in nonage, or otherwise young and unskilful,
were never able to defend his patrimony, being his no longer
than he can hold it by force of arms. But by that time he grow
to a competent age, and have buried an uncle or two, he also
taketh his turn, and leaveth it in like order to his posterity.
This custom breedeth among them continual wars and treasons.

From Edmund Campion, *History of Ireland*, ch. vi, in (**17**), p. 316.

Cuttings and Spendings of Irish lords

*As the Gaelic lords could not wholly maintain themselves from the mensal
lands allocated to them they supplemented their real incomes by billeting
themselves and their entourage on their tenants and subchiefs. On a small
scale this was like the progresses of medieval kings, or lesser lords
moving from one manor to another. The system was summarised by the
motto 'Spend me and defend me' although it is clear that, regarded as a
method of raising revenue and of arranging local defence, it was both
arbitrary and oppressive. The tenant never knew precisely how much he
would be mulcted, while the lord frequently had to have recourse to the
'strong arm' to secure his rights.*

Bonaght is of two sorts: bonaght-bonny and bonaght-beg.
Bonaght-bonny is a certain payment or allowance made unto
her Majesty's gallowglass or kerne by the Irishry only, who are

107

severally bound to yield a yearly proportion of victuals and money, of their finding, everyone according to his ability, so that the kerne and gallowglass are kept all the year by the Irishry, and divided at times between them. Bonaght-beg, or little bonaght, is a proportion of money, rateably charged upon every ploughland, towards the finding of the gallowglass. . . .

Of the second sort, Coyne is as much to say as a placing of men and boys upon the country, used by a prerogative of the Brehon law, whereby they are permitted to take meat, drink, *aqua vitae* and money of their hosts, without pay-making therefore. As many as keep idle men, take it outrageously where they come, and by the custom of the country it was lawful to place themselves upon whom they would. It is the beggaring of the country and an intolerable evil without measure. Livery is horsemeat, exacted for the horses of those which take coyne, or otherwise send them to the poor tenants to be fed. The tenant must find the horses and boys and give them as much corn and sheaf-oats, wheat and barley as they will have. . . .

Coshery is certain feasts which the lord useth to take of his tenants after Easter, Christmas, Whitsuntide, Michaelmas and all other times at his pleasure; he goeth to their houses with all his train and idle men of his country, and leaveth them not till all they have be spent, and consumed, and holdeth on this course till he have visited all his tenants one after another.

From John Dymmok, *A Treatise of Ireland*, in (**17**), pp. 328–9.

document 3

Shane O'Neill in London

Shane's visit to London was the result of the government's desire to secure his submission to the Crown, and his own desire to strengthen his position in Ulster by securing the grant of the earldom of Tyrone. In short, it was to be a repetition of Con O'Neill's visit to London in 1542. But between father and son there were substantial differences. Con forsook the name of O'Neill, promised to use English, swore to obey English law, adopted English clothing and became Earl of Tyrone. Shane flaunted himself as a proud Gaelic chieftain, regarded English law and English habits with contempt and was not belted with the desired earldom. Strangely, his safe-conduct was honoured and he returned from this confrontation of the contrasting Gaelic and Elizabethan societies to become the architect of his own violent end.

And now Shane O'Neill came from Ireland, to keep the promise he had made a year before with an escort of gallowglass, armed with battle-axes, bare-headed, with flowing curls, yellow shirts dyed with saffron ... large sleeves, short tunics and rough cloaks, whom the English followed with as much wonderment as if they had come from China or America. O'Neill was received with all kindness, and throwing himself at the Queen's feet he owned with lamentation his crime of rebellion and begged for pardon. When asked with courtesy by what right he had excluded Hugh his brother Matthew's son from his ancestral lands, he replied boldly, as he had done in Ireland, 'By the best of right. For I,' he said, 'as the true and legitimate son and heir of Con, born of his lawful wife, have entered upon my father's estate. Matthew was the son of a blacksmith of Dundalk, not true born, but born after Con's marriage with his wife Alison, and craftily passed off on Con by the mother as his son, so as to cheat me of the possessions and title of O'Neill. . . . But I am the true heir by the law of God and man, being the first son of my father born in lawful wedlock, and called O'Neill by the common consent of chiefs and people according to the law of our ancestors called tanistry, by which the man grown is to be preferred before the boy, and the uncle to his nephew whose grandfather has outlived his father. . . .'

So the Queen believed his tale, and he was sent home with honour and for some time served well and loyally against the robbers of the Hebrides.

From William Camden, *Annales rerum Anglicarum et Hibernicarum . . .,* in (**17**), pp. 171–2.

document 4
Captain Cuellar's Account of the Gaelic Irish

It was not only to English observers that Gaelic society appeared to be both backward and barbaric. Cuellar was an Armada survivor whose adventures led him through parts of Sligo and Leitrim, then, as now, among the poorest and least developed areas of Ireland. There Gaelic society had been less affected by outside influences than elsewhere. Like an Elizabethan adventurer or an Anglo-Irish gentleman Cuellar regarded those native Irish he met as savages: 'They were the first to rob us and strip to the skin those who came alive to land.' He was astonished to find that they were practising Catholics, and that the educated minority spoke Latin!

The custom of these savages is to live as the brute beasts among the mountains, which are very rugged in that part of Ireland where we lost ourselves. They live in huts made of straw. The men are all large bodied, and of handsome features and limbs; and as active as the roe-deer. They do not eat oftener than once a day, and this is at night; and that which they usually eat is butter with oaten bread. They drink sour milk, for they have no other drink; they don't drink water, although it is the best in the world. On feast days they eat some flesh half-cooked, without bread or salt, as that is their custom. They clothe themselves, according to their habit, with tight trousers and short loose coats of very coarse goat's hair. They cover themselves with blankets and wear their hair down to their eyes. They are great walkers, and inured to toil. They carry on perpetual war with the English, who here keep garrison for the Queen, from whom they defend themselves, and do not let them enter their territory, which is subject to inundation, and marshy. That district extends for more than forty leagues in length and breadth. The chief inclination of these people is to be robbers, and to plunder each other; so that no day passes without a call to arms among them. For the people in one village becoming aware that in another there are cattle, or other effects, they immediately come armed in the night, and 'go Santiago' [attack], and kill one another; and the English from the garrisons, getting to know who had taken, and robbed, most cattle, then come down upon them, and carry away the plunder. They have, therefore, no other remedy but to withdraw themselves to the mountains, with their women and cattle; for they possess no other property, nor more moveables nor clothing. They sleep upon the ground, on rushes, newly cut and full of water and ice.

110

The most of the women are very beautiful, but badly dressed [got up]. They do not wear more than a chemise, and a blanket, with which they cover themselves, and a linen cloth, much doubled, over the head, and tied in front. They are great workers and housekeepers, after their fashion. These people call themselves Christians. Mass is said among them, and regulated according to the orders of the Church of Rome. The great majority of their churches, monasteries, and hermitages, have been demolished by the hands of the English, who are in garrison, and of those natives who have joined them, and are as bad as they. In short, in this kingdom their is neither justice nor right, and everyone does what he pleases.

From *Captain Cuellar's narrative* (**77**), pp. 61–2.

document 5

Brehon law

In this extract Sir John Davies, Solicitor-General for Ireland, and subsequently Attorney-General, under James I, points to the brehon law as the main weakness of Gaelic society, which collapsed with the defeat of Hugh O'Neill.

For, if we consider the nature of the Irish customs, we shall find that the people which doth use them must of necessity be rebels to all good government, destroy the commonwealth wherein they live, and bring barbarism and desolation upon the richest and most fruitful land of the world. For, whereas by the just and honourable law of England, and by the laws of all other well-governed kingdoms and commonweals, murder, manslaughter, rape, robbery, and theft are punished with death, by the Irish custom, or Brehon Law, the highest of these offences was punished only by fine, which they called an ericke. . . . As for oppression, extortion, and other trespasses, the weaker had never any remedy against the stronger; whereby it came to pass that no man could enjoy his life, his wife, his lands or goods in safety if a mightier man than himself had an appetite to take the same from him. Wherein they were little better than cannibals, who do hunt one another, and he that hath most strength and swiftness doth eat and devour all his fellows. . . . These two Irish customs [tanistry and gavelkind] made all their properties uncertain, being shuffled and changed and removed so often from one to another by new elections and partitions, which uncertainty of estates hath been the true cause of such desolation and barbarism in this land . . . for though the Irishry be a nation of great antiquity and wanted neither wit nor valour, and though they had received the Christian faith above twelve hundred years since, and were lovers of music, poetry, and all kind of learning, and possessed a land abounding with all things necessary for the civil life of man, yet, which is strange to be related, they did never build any houses of brick or stone, some few poor religious houses excepted, before the reign of King Henry the Second. . . . Neither did any of them in all this time plant any gardens or orchards, enclose or improve their lands, live together in settles villages or towns, nor make any provision for posterity, which, being against all commonsense and reason, must needs be imputed to those unreasonable customs which made their estates so uncertain and transitory in their possessions.

From Sir John Davies, *A Discovery of The True Causes why Ireland was never entirely subdued*, in (**21**), pp. 290–2.

II. THE EXTENSION OF ENGLISH LAW

document 6

Poynings' Law, 1494

The purpose of this law was to bring the Parliament of the Lordship of Ireland under royal control, and to make certain that it would remain subordinate to the English administration. The Irish Parliament could only pass bills which had been approved by the Privy Council in London. This machinery ensured a subordinate and 'colonial' role for the Irish parliament, and prevented the Anglo-Irish lords from dominating it for their own purposes. It was not until 1698, when William Molyneux published his pamphlet 'The Case of Ireland's being bound by Acts of Parliament in England, stated', that the opinion was voiced that the only true authority in Ireland was that of the King, Lords and Commons of Ireland. Poynings' Law was repealed in 1782 and the Irish Parliament entered upon a brief but remarkable interlude before it was suppressed under the Act of Union, 1800.

An act that no parliament be holden in this land until the acts be certified into England

Item, at the request of the commons of the land of Ireland, be it ordained, enacted and established, that at the next parliament that there shall be holden by the king's commandment and licence, wherein amongst other, the king's grace intendeth to have a general resumption of his whole revenues since the last day of the reign of King Edward the second, no parliament be holden hereafter in the said land, but at such season as the king's lieutenant and council there first do certify the king, under the great seal of that land, the causes and considerations, and all such acts as them seemeth should pass in the same parliament, and such causes, considerations, and acts, affirmed by the king and his council to be good and expedient for that land, and his licence thereupon, as well in affirmation of the said causes and acts, as to summon the said parliament, under his great seal of England had and obtained; that done, a parliament to be had and holden after the form and effect afore rehearsed: and if any parliament be holden in that land hereafter, contrary to the form and provision aforesaid, it be deemed void and of none effect in law.

From *Irish Historical Documents 1172–1922* (**16**), p. 83.

document 7
'Sober ways, politic drifts and amiable persuasions'
—Letter from Henry VIII to the Earl of Surrey, 1520

Henry VIII wished to play a part on the European stage and could not afford to become too much involved in Irish affairs. Just as Henry VII laid the legal foundations for English supremacy by sending over Sir Edward Poynings, and subsequently handing over the effective government of the country to the earl of Kildare, so Henry VIII hoped that, by the 'politic drift' of 'surrender and re-grant' he could induce the Irish and Anglo-Irish nobles to adopt English law. However, this early

113

Tudor policy was forced to give way to more vigorous policies of plantation and conquest under Henry's two daughters.

We, and our Council think and verily believe, that in case circumspect and politic ways be used, ye shall not only bring them [the 'captains' or chiefs of Irish lordships] to further obedience, for the observance of our laws, and governing themselves according to the same, but also following justice, to forbear to detain rebelliously such lands and dominions as to us in right apperaineth; which thing must as yet rather be practised by sober ways, politic drifts, and amiable persuasions, founded in law and reason, than by rigorous dealing, commina-tions, or any other enforcement by strength or violence. And, to be plain unto you, to spend so much money for the reduction of that land, to bring the Irishry in appearance only of obeisance, without that they should observe our laws, and resort to our courts for justice, and restore such dominions as they unlawfully detain from us; it were a thing of little policy, less advantage, and least effect.

From S.P. Hen. VIII, ii, 52–4, in (**17**), pp. 103–5.

document 8

The kingdom of Ireland

This act was a necessary consequence of the Reformation changes in England, for the medieval lordship based on a Papal grant would no longer be maintained. It also gave expression to the growing intervention by the Crown in Ireland since 1534. However, it was not until after the death of Elizabeth that the whole of Ireland became effective shire-ground, and Ireland was united for the first time in history. The kingdom established by Henry VIII was ended by the Act of Union, 1800, by which Great Britain and Ireland were formed into a United Kingdom.

AN ACT THAT THE KING AND HIS SUCCESSORS BE
KINGS OF IRELAND

An act that the king of England, his heirs and his successors be kings of Ireland

Forasmuch as the king our most gracious dread sovereign lord, and his grace's most noble progenitors, kings of England, have been lords of this land of Ireland, having all manner kingly jurisdiction, power, pre-eminence, and authority royal, belonging or appertaining to the royal estate and majesty of a king, by the name of lords of Ireland, where the king's majesty, and his most noble progenitors, justly and rightfully were, and of right ought to be kings of Ireland, and so to be reputed, taken, named and called, and for lack of naming the king's majesty and his noble progenitors kings of Ireland, according to their said true and just title, style and name therein, hath been great occasion that the Irish men and inhabitants within this realm of Ireland have not been so obedient to the king's highness and his most noble progenitors, and to their laws, as they of right, and according to their allegiance and bounden duties ought to have been. Wherefore, at the humble pursuit, petition, and request of the lords spiritual and temporal, and other the king's loving, faithful and obedient subjects of this his land of Ireland, and by their full assents, be it enacted, ordained, and established by authority of this present parliament, that the king's highness, his heirs and successors, kings of England, be always kings of this land of Ireland, and that his majesty, his heirs and successors, have the name, style, title, and honour of king of this land of Ireland, with all manner honours, pre-eminences, prerogatives, dignities, and other things, whatsoever they be, to the estate and majesty of a king imperial appertaining or belonging; and that his majesty, his heirs and successors, be from henceforth named, called, accepted, reputed, and taken to be kings of this land of Ireland, to have, hold, and enjoy the said style, title, majesty, and honours of king of Ireland, with all manner pre-eminences, prerogatives, dignities and all other the premises, unto the king's highness, his heirs and successors for ever, as united and knit to the imperial crown of the realm of England.

From *Irish Historical Documents 1172–1922* (**16**), p. 77.

The Attainder of Shane O'Neill

document 9

This act was not only a blast of the trumpet against the specific Gaelic title of The O'Neill, but was also, by implication, a legal attack on all similar titles. This was an inevitable concomitant of the extension of English law, for such law, with its emphasis on primogeniture and on all titles deriving ultimately from the Crown, was in direct conflict with brehon law. Curiously enough, this act was not invoked when Turlough Luineach O'Neill, Shane's successor, became The O'Neill.

Forasmuch as the name of the O'Neill, in the judgements of the uncivil people of this Realm, doth carry in itself so great a sovereignty, as they suppose that all the lords and people of Ulster should rather live in servitude to that name, than in subjection to the crown of England: be it therefore, by your Majesty, with the assent of the lords spiritual and temporal, and the Commons in this present Parliament assembled, and by the authority of the same, that the same name of O'Neill, with the manner and ceremonies of his creation, and all the superiorities, titles, dignities, pre-eminences, jurisdictions, authorities, rules, tributes, and expenses, used, claimed, usurped, or taken by any O'Neill, as in right of that name, or otherwise, from the beginning, of any the lords, captains, or people of Ulster, and all manner of offices given by the said O'Neill, shall from henceforth cease, end, determine, and be utterly abolished and extinct for ever. And that what person soever he be that shall hereafter challenge, execute, or take upon him that name of O'Neill, or any superiority, dignity, pre-eminence and jurisdiction, authority, rule, tributes, or expenses, used, claimed, usurped, or taken heretofore by any O'Neill, of the lords, captains, or people of Ulster, the same shall be deemed, adjudged, and taken high treason against your Majesty, your crown and dignity: and the person or persons therein offending, and being thereof attainted, shall suffer and sustain such pains of death, forfeiture of lands and goods, as in cases of high treason by the law of this Realm hath been accustomed and used.

From *Contemporary Sources 1509–1610* (**17**), p. 174.

116

Palatine jurisdiction

*The palatinates in Ormond or Tipperary under the Butlers and in
Kerry under the Geraldines of Desmond were originally marcher lordships, comparable to those on the borders of Wales or that granted to the
Bishop of Durham. By the sixteenth century such a type of devolution
was obsolete, and in England and Wales the marcher lordships were
replaced by special Councils acting under the direction of the Privy
Council in London. Similarly, in Ireland the palatine jurisdiction of Kerry
was terminated when the Presidency of Munster was set up in 1570.
Tipperary lingered on, to become, according to Spenser, a sort of Alsatia
for lawbreakers.*

EUDOX. I would gladly know what you call a County Palatine,
and whence it is so called.

IREN. It was, I suppose, first named Palatine of a pale, as it
were a pale and defence to their inward lands, so as it is called
the English Pale; and therefore is a Palsgrave named an Earl
Palatine. Others think of the Latin *palare;* that is, to forage or
outrun, because those marchers and borderers used commonly so
to do. So as to have a County Palatine is, in effect, to have a
privilege to spoil the enemies' borders adjoining. And surely so
it is used at this day, as a privilege place of spoils and stealths;
for the county of Tipperary, which is now the only County
Palatine in Ireland, is by abuse of some bad ones made a
receptacle to rob the rest of the counties about it, by means of
whose privileges none will follow their stealths: so as it, being
situate in the very lap of all the land, is made now a border;
which how inconvenient it is let every man judge.

From Edmund Spenser, *A View of The State of Ireland* in (**21**), p. 66.

The Presidency of Munster

*The Presidencies of Munster and Connacht were both a conciliar form of
local administration under the control of the Lord Deputy and Council in
Dublin. Essentially such a form of government was a temporary*

expedient until the whole kingdom was effectively 'reduced to civility'
under James I. Not until the establishment of the Congested Districts
Board in the 1890s were the particular needs of substantial areas of
Munster, Connacht and western Ulster to become again the concern of a
specialised government agency.

13. Item where also the said lord president and council, or two of them at the least, whereof the lord president to be one, hath full power and authority, by letters patent under the great seal of this realm, to execute the martial law, when necessity shall require, in as large and ample manner as to any other it hath been accustomed to be granted within this realm of Ireland, the said lord president and council shall have good regard thereto, that no use be of the martial law, but where mere necessity shall require, for the exercise thereof is only to be allowed where other ordinary administration of justice by law cannot assume place; foreseeing always, that no party having five pounds of freehold, or goods to the value of forty pounds, shall be tried by the order of the martial law, but by order of the common law, and yet, if necessity, for service and terror to others, shall at any time require to execute the martial law upon any one person or more, being of greater value in lands or goods than above is expressed, the president, in such special cases, may use his discretion, and thereof and of the causes that moved him, shall make us the lord deputy of the realm privy.

14. Item, it is and shall be lawful for the lord president and council, or to any two of them whereof the lord president to be one, to prosecute and oppress any rebel or rebels with swords and with fire; and for the doing of the same, to levy in warlike manner and array, and with the same to march such and so many of the queen's highness's subjects, as to his discretion shall seem convenient; and if that any castle, pile, or house, be with force kept against them, it shall be lawful for the said lord president and council, or two of them, whereof the lord president to be one, to bring before any such castle, pile, or house, so to be kept against them, any of the queen's majesty's ordnance and great artillery. . . .

15. And it is ordered by the said lord deputy and council, that if any person complain to the said lord president and council, and that they shall think their complaints worthy the hearing,

that the persons so complained upon, shall be sent for by a letter missive under the queen's signet, to appear before the lord president and council at a day and place by them to be appointed, there to answer to such things as shall be laid to their charge. . . .

17. And the said lord president and council, according to their commission, shall have power and authority by these presents, diligently to hear, determine and try all and all manner of extortions, maintenance, embraceries, and oppressions, conspiracies, rescues, escapes, corruptions, falsehoods, and all other evil doings, defaults and misdemeanours of all sheriffs, justices of peace, mayors, sovereigns, portreeves, bailiffs, stewards, lieutenants, escheators, coroners, gaolers, clerks, and other officers and ministers of justice, and their deputies, as well in all the counties and countries within the province of Munster aforesaid, and within the supposed liberties of Tipperary and Kerry, as in all cities and other towns corporate within the limits of their said commission, of what degree soever they be, and punish the same according to the quality and quantity of their offence, by their discretions, leaving nevertheless to the lords and owners of all lawful liberties such profits as they may lawfully claim.

From *Irish Historical Documents 1172–1922* (**16**), pp. 113–14.

Composition for cess in Connacht

document 12

It was government policy to reduce disorder and extend the rule of law by encouraging the replacement of the arbitrary exactions of the Gaelic lords—their 'cuttings and spendings'—by precise money rents. This process of composition was applied to the Pale in lieu of cess; it was applied in parts of Munster after the downfall of the Desmonds, and the entire province of Connacht was visited by Commissioners who enquired into the ownership of landed property and defined the rents to be paid. A further composition was arranged in 1591 when land ownership in Monaghan was settled principally between nine branches of the MacMahons. Rents were stabilised and although, as in Mayo, disorder did not disappear completely, yet Monaghan was able to be excluded from the confiscation and plantation under James I. Hugh O'Neill was right to suppose that this composition of Monaghan was as much an attack on the Gaelic order as the seizure of Enniskillen castle.

Commission from the Queen to Sir Richard Bingham, Chief Commissioner in Connaught and Thomond; the Archbishop of Tome (Tuam); the Earls of Ormond and Clanricard; the Bishop[s] of Clonfert and Elphine; the Lord Brimigham, Baron of Athenry; Sir Nicholas White, Master of the Rolls; Sir Edward Waterhouse, one of the Privy Council; Sir Thomas Lestrange, one of the same; Thomas Dillon, Chief Justice of the said province; Charles Calthorp, Attorney-General; Gerald Quemerford, Attorney in the said province; Sir Tirrelagh O'Brien; Sir Donell O'Connor Sligo; Sir Brien O'Rorck; Sir Richard Bourck; Sir Morogh ne Dowe O'Flaerty; Francis Barkley, Provost-Marshal in the said province; Nicholas Fitz Symons, of Dublin, alderman; John Marbury; Robert Fowle; and John Browne.

Whereas the said province is torn by the dissensions of the lords and chieftains, who challenge authorities, cuttings, and cessings, under pretext of defending the people under their rules; and we understand that these our subjects are inclined, through the ministry of Sir John Perrot, our Deputy General, to embrace all good ways and means to conserve them in obedience, whereby our prerogative may be known, and their rights and titles made certain: We authorize you to call before you all the nobility, spiritual and temporal, and all the chieftains and lords of the countries, and thereupon, in lieu of the uncertain cesse borne to us and of the cutting[s] and spendings of the lords, to compound for a rent certain to us upon every quarter or quantity of land within that province. The baronies to be divided into manors.

Witness our said Lord Deputy General, at Dublin, 15 July, 27 Eliz.

II. THE RETURN OF THE COMMISSIONERS

By our own view, and by the presentments of good and lawful men, we have found what number of quarters of land are

120

contained within the counties of Clare, Galway, Mayo, Sligo, Rosscommon, and the confines thereof, within Connaught and Thomond, accompting O'Rorck's country to be of the same, as in the several presentments taken thereof is at large inserted, which we return, together with the several indentures passed and agreed upon for the composition rent granted in the same to the Queen by the lords, freeholders, &c.

Dated 3 October, 27 Eliz.

The barony of Clancoistolla is not as yet presented, nor comprised within this composition.

Signed by Sir Richard Bingham and others.

From *Calendar of Carew MSS, 1575–88* (**19**), p. 405.

Capture of Red Hugh O'Donnell

document 13

It is curious to reflect that the Dublin administration, which was concerned with the extension of Common Law over the whole of Ireland, should itself have adopted the primitive Gaelic expedient of keeping hostages as guarantors for their kinsmen's good behaviour. This filibustering action by Perrot largely put an end to the tacit alliance between the government and the O'Donnells, although it did not prevent Niall Garve O'Donnell rendering useful service to the Crown in the campaigns against Hugh O'Neill.

The Lord Deputie's Devise was thus. He had prepared a Shippe with some Wines to be sent into *O-Donell's* Contry, and the Captayne of that Shippe beinge one chosen to the Porpose, had this geiven hym in Command from the Lord Deputy, that when he came into *O-Donell's* Contry, he should sayle as neere his Dwelling as he might, and there profferre his Wines to be solde (beinge *Sackes* which the *Irishmen* love best) and soe he did. At his Coming into the Contry, the Contry People came to the Shippe, some to drink, some to prise the Wines, and all of them, according to the Captayne's Instructions, had what Wine they would drinke for nothinge, as a Taste, with this kinde Offer, that if *O-Donell* would come hymselfe, he should buy the best Wine at a reasonable Rate. At length *O-Donell* came hymselfe to

121

buy some Wines, whom they used so courteously, that they gave hym his full Allowance, and finding hym well fraughted, and the Windes servinge well for that Porpose that they came, to returne backe, and to carie *O-Donell* with them, they stowed hym under Hatches at the first, and soe brought him to *Dublyn*, without Stroake or Losse of any Man's Life. Which to have byn effected by Force, as it was first intended, would by all Conjecture of Reason have cost the Queene much Treasure, if not Blood of hir Subjectes, because *O-Donell* at that time was one of the strongest, and most dangerous Subjectes in that Kingdome, by reason of his Alliance, his Command, and the Strength of his Contrie; but by this Stratagem he was brought in without Blowes, and his Contrie kept in Quiett without any Rebellion.

From *The History of Sir John Perrot* (**26**), pp. 278–80.

document 14
Proclamation of the supremacy of English law, 1605

Sir Arthur Chichester's Proclamation in 1605 represented the culmination of all the efforts to extend English law under Elizabeth and the early Tudors. Ireland was now united, shired and the public peace now proclaimed was enforced by regular circuits of judges on assize. All were now equally subjects of the Crown; as Sir John Davies expressed it: 'There is no nation of people under the sun that doth love equal and indifferent justice better than the Irish.'

We do therefore in his Majesty's name, straightly charge and command all and every the said lords and owners, that they and every of them do forthwith so dispose of their said lands, as they may receive certain rents and certain duties for the same, and that they and every of them do from henceforth utterly forbear to use or usurp upon any of their tenants or dependents those odious and unlawful customs of cutting and coshering: which customs we will and command to be discontinued and abolished for ever in this Kingdom, as being barbarous, unreasonable, and intolerable in any civil or Christian commonwealth. . . . and to the end the said poor tenants and inhabitants, and every of them, may from henceforth know and understand that free estate and condition wherein they were born, and wherein from henceforth they shall all be continued and maintained, we do by this present proclamation in his Majesty's name declare and publish, that they and every of them, their wives and children, are the free, natural, and immediate subjects of his Majesty, and are not to be reputed or called the natives or natural followers of any other lord or chieftain whatsoever, and that they and every of them ought to depend wholly and immediately upon his Majesty, who is both able and willing to protect them, and not upon any other inferior lord or lords. . .

And we do further declare and publish unto all his Majesty's loving subjects, that (notwithstanding this gracious proclamation) his Majesty will no longer continue his protection over them or any of them, than they and every of them shall continue in their loyalty and obedience, and depend wholly upon his Majesty and his laws, from which if they or any of them shall hereafter make any defection, his Majesty is fully resolved to extend the uttermost rigour of his laws against them, without any pardon or remission, and to prosecute them and every of them by all ways and means possible, to the utter extirping and rooting out of them, their names and generations, for ever. And lastly, we do will and require such and so many of his Majesty's poor and inferior sort of subjects, as shall from time to time be grieved or burdened with any oppression, exaction, or other insolence of any of the said great lords or gentlemen . . . that they eftsoons make their complaint either to the Justices of Assize being present in their several circuits, or in their absence to the Governor of the country or sheriff of the county wherein they dwell. And thereupon we will and command every governor or sheriff within each particular country and county to examine such wrongs and injuries so complained of, and the circumstances thereof, and the same forthwith to certify either to the Justices of Assize when they shall come in their circuits, or unto us the Lord Deputy and Council, to the end redress may be given to the parties grieved, and punishment inflicted upon the offenders.

From *Contemporary Sources 1509–1610* (**17**), pp. 208–10.

III. CATHOLIC AND PROTESTANT

document 15

The Act of Uniformity, 1560

This act represented the importation of the 'Elizabethan compromise' into Irish ecclesiastical affairs. It remained a dead letter over most of Ireland, for even in the Pale the strength of recusant opinion among the Anglo-Irish made a temporising policy inevitable. Not until the seventeenth century did the religious problem begin to assume its modern forms.

Where at the death of our late sovereign lord King Edward VI there remained one uniform order of common service, prayer and the administration of sacraments, rites and ceremonies in the church of England, which was set forth in one book entitled 'The book of common prayer, and administration of sacraments, and other rites and ceremonies in the church of England' authorized by act of parliament, holden in the said realm of England, in the fifth and sixth years of our late sovereign lord King Edward VI entitled, *An act for the uniformity of common prayer and the administration of the sacraments*, which was repealed and taken away by act of parliament in the said realm of England in the reign of our late sovereign lady Queen Mary, to the great decay of the true honour of God, and discomfort to the professors of the truth of Christ's religion, be it therefore enacted . . . that the said book with the order of service, and of the administration of sacraments, rites and ceremonies, with the alterations and additions therein added and appointed by this statute, shall stand and be from and after the feast of Pentecost next ensuing in full force and effect, . . .
II. And further be it enacted . . . that all and singular ministers in any cathedral or parish church, or other place within this realm of Ireland, shall from and after the feast of Saint John Baptist then next ensuing, be bounder to say and use the matins, evensong, celebration of the lord's supper, and administration of each of the sacraments, in all their common and open prayer, in such order and form as is mentioned in the said book.
III. . . . from and after the said feast of Saint John Baptist all and every person and persons inhabiting within this realm shall

diligently and faithfully, having no lawful or reasonable excuse to be absent, endeavour themselves to resort to their parish church or chapel accustomed, or upon reasonable let thereof to some usual place, where common prayer and such service of God shall be used in such time of let, upon every Sunday and other days ordained and used to be kept as holy days, and then and there to abide orderly and soberly during the time of common prayer, preachings or other service of God, there to be used and ministered, upon pain of punishment by the censures of the church, and also upon pain that every person so offending shall forfeit for every such offence twelve pence to be levied by the churchwarden of the parish where such offence shall be done to the use of the poor of the same parish, of the goods, lands, and tenements of such offender by way of distress; and for the due execution thereof the queen's most excellent majesty, the lords temporal, and all the commons in this present parliament assembled, do in God's name earnestly require and charge all archbishops, bishops, and other ordinaries, that they shall endeavour themselves to the uttermost of their knowledge that the due execution hereof may be had throughout their dioceses and charges. . . .

From *Irish Historical Documents 1172–1922* (**16**), pp. 121–3.

document 16
Spenser's view of the clergy

In Ireland, as in Poland and Bohemia, the forces of the Counter-Reformation were zealously at work, contrasting, as Edmund Spenser saw, with the 'politique' and cool approach of the conforming clergy. The zeal of Dr Nicholas Sanders or of Archbishop Dermot O'Hurley (martyred in 1583) contributed to as definite a result in Ireland as did the work of John Knox in Scotland.

Wherein it is great wonder to see the odds which are between the zeal of Popish priests and the ministers of the Gospel. For they spare not to come out of Spain, from Rome and from Rheims, by long toil and dangerous travelling hither, where they know peril of death awaiteth them and no reward or riches are to be found, only to draw the people unto the Church of Rome: whereas some of our idle ministers, having a way for credit and estimation thereby opened unto them, and having the livings of the country offered unto them without pains and without peril, will neither for the same, nor any love of God, nor zeal of religion, nor for all the good they may do by winning souls to God, be drawn forth from their warm nests to look out into God's harvest, which is even ready for the sickle and all the fields yellow long ago.

From Edmund Spenser, *A View of the State of Ireland* in (**21**), p. 203.

document 17
James Fitzmaurice's Proclamation, 1579

In issuing this battle cry of the Counter-Reformation James Fitzmaurice was first, satisfying his sponsorship by the Papacy, second, endeavouring to drum up practical support from Spain and France, and, third, by stressing that he was not rebelling against the Crown, but against a heretic Queen, was hoping to appeal for support amongst the Anglo-Irish. In all these objectives he failed, largely because rebellion in Elizabeth's reign had more to do with land ownership than religious idealism.

This war is undertaken for the defence of the Catholic religion against the heretics. Pope Gregory XIII hath chosen us for general captain in this same war, as it appeareth at large by his own letters patent, which thing he did so much rather because his predecessor Pope Pius V had before deprived Elizabeth, the patroness of the aforesaid heresies, of all royal power and dominion, as it is plainly declared by his declaratory sentence, the authentic copy whereof we also have to show. Therefore now we fight not against the lawful sceptre and honourable throne of England, but against a tyrant which refuseth to hear Christ speaking by his vicar.

From *Contemporary Sources 1509–1610* (**17**), p. 169.

Correspondence between the Earl of Tyrone and Philip II of Spain

These letters reveal how Hugh O'Neill endeavoured to identify the last stand of the Gaelic order with the Counter-Reformation, and how political considerations prevented Philip II from becoming too deeply involved in Irish affairs. Precisely the same considerations prevented Elizabeth from committing herself too far in the revolt of the United Provinces.

THE EARL OF TYRONE AND O'DONNELL TO THE KING OF SPAIN

Our only hope of re-establishing the Catholic religion rests on your assistance. Now or never our Church must be succoured. By the timidity or negligence of the messengers our former letters have not reached you. We therefore again beseech you to send us 2,000 or 3,000 soldiers, with money and arms, before the feast of St. Philip and St. James. With such aid we hope to restore the faith of the Church, and to secure you a kingdom.

5. Cal. Octobris 1595.

Signed: O'Neill, Hugh O'Donnell.

'Intercepted, and received the 29th Sept. 1595, from the hands of Piers O'Cullen.'

PHILIP II, KING OF SPAIN, TO THE EARL OF TYRONE.

I have been informed you are defending the Catholic cause against the English. That this is acceptable to God is proved by the signal victories which you have gained. I hope you will continue to prosper; and you need not doubt but I will render you any assistance you may require. Give credence to Fussius, the bearer, and acquaint him with your affairs and your wishes.

Madrid, 22 January 1596.

Headed: 'A letter sent to the Earl of Tyrone from the King of Spain, delivered by Alonso Cobos; which letter the Earl sent to the Lord Deputy and Council, taking Captain William Warren's promise, and his servant's oath who brought it, that no copy should be taken of it.'

From *Calendar of Carew MSS 1589–1600* (**19**), pp. 122, 141.

Proclamation against toleration in Ireland, 1605

*The consequence of the Elizabethan conquest and the enforcement of
English law over the whole kingdom of Ireland was that the state was
now in a position to insist on the substantive application of the Elizabethan
Church settlement. This proclamation was to Irish Catholics what the
Hampton Court Conference was to the Presbyterians and other dissenters
in England.*

[James I] is informed that his subjects in the Realm of Ireland
have since the decease of Queen Elizabeth, been much abused
by an untrue suggestion and report to the effect that he purposes
to give liberty of conscience or toleration of religion to his
subjects in that Kingdom, contrary to the express laws and
statutes therein enacted, and to that uniformity of religion
which has ever been constantly professed by him and is
universally used and observed in his other dominions and
countries. This false rumour is not only a secret imputation
upon him, as if he were more remiss or less careful in the
government of the Church of Ireland than of those other
Churches whereof he has the supreme charge, but also divers of
his subjects in that Kingdom are heartened and encouraged to
continue in their superstition and recusancy; and such Jesuits,
seminary priests, and other priests and bishops ordained by
foreign authority, as did secretly before lurk in sundry parts of
that Realm, do now more boldly and presumptuously show and
declare themselves in the use and exercise of their functions,
and in contempt of the King, his laws and religion. He has
therefore thought meet to declare and publish to all his loving
subjects in the Realm of Ireland his high displeasure with the
report and rumour, and with the authors and spreaders thereof,
and his resolve never to do any act that may confirm the hopes
of any creature, that they shall ever have from him any toleration to exercise any other religion than that which is agreeable
to God's Word, and is established by the laws of the Realm.
By this public act he desires to declare to all his subjects his
resolution; and he straightly admonishes and commands those
of that Realm from henceforth duly to resort and come to their
several parish churches or chapels, to hear divine service every

Sunday and Holy Day, according to the tenor and intent of the laws and statutes, upon the pains and penalties contained therein, which he will have from henceforth duly put into execution.

From *Contemporary Sources 1509–1610* (**17**), pp. 143–4.

IV. MILITARY AFFAIRS

document 20

The capture of Carrigafoyle Castle, March 1580

This letter from the Lord Deputy Pelham to the Lords of the Council in England indicates the ruthlessness and ferocity of warfare in sixteenth-century Ireland, a ferocity foreshadowed by the notorious Pardon of Maynooth in 1535, by which the garrison of the castle were executed after they had surrendered. In mitigation it should be said that Ireland was one of Europe's frontiers, like that against the Turk, or in the New World, where the accepted rules of warfare were not always observed.

On the 25th, having met here with all the shipping, I encamped before this place, where Ormond came to me two days after. As the house was circuited with the sea, it was not to be attempted but with the cannon; and because in the ships that brought the ordnance the victuals lay upon the pieces, I was forced to spend three or four days before I could unlade and plant the battery. The ward consisted of 16 Spaniards and 50 others under one Captain Julian, who reported himself to be an excellent engineer, and undertook the keeping of it at the request of the Countess of Desmond, as appears by a Spanish letter written in her name by Doctor Sanders. They railed against her Majesty, and declared that they kept the castle for the King of Spain. I planted the battery so as to make the fall of the house to fill the ditch of the barbican. We battered it on Tuesday for six hours, and this day from morning till two of the clock after noon, before the house fell, but in the fall, the ditch and flankers being choked, it became forthwith assaultable. Captain Mackeworth entered the outer banne, and was master of it presently. The Spaniards retired to a turret upon the wall of the barbican, and some into the vaults. Some of the Irish and one Englishman, a rebel, attempting to escape by swimming, were slain. Upon a shot or two part of the Spaniards left the turret, and were executed. Only Captain Julian and six other Spaniards and certain women submitted themselves to Captain Mackeworth. All were presently hanged saving the captain whom I keep for a day or two to learn what is intended, and how they have been succoured and relieved. Three soldiers were slain, and three persons hurt; among the latter, Sir William Stanlie. 'Many gentlemen put themselves into the place that had little thanks of me, namely, Mr Zouche; for every man had a desire to salute the Spaniards.'

Ormond and I have been evil assisted with such as have been trusted for spial upon the rebels. The Chief Baron (Sir Lucas Dillon) has accompanied me all this journey. Sir Nicholas Malbie has drawn himself into these parts of Thomond, and lodges in the island of Ineskattie, to relieve the army with supplies out of his government. Mr. Treasurer (Sir Henry Wallop), forced by sickness to remain at Limerick, 'so disposeth of the victuals that come from thence as doth much further these proceedings.'

From *Calendar of Carew MSS 1575–88* (**19**), pp. 237–8.

document 2

The Spanish Armada

Fresh interest in the Armada wrecks off the Irish coast has been created by the location of the galleass 'Girona' off the Giant's Causeway, co. Antrim, by the Belgian diver Robert Sténuit. Breechblocks, cannonballs, ingots of lead, coins and jewellery have been salvaged in one of the most impressive treasure troves of modern times in the British Isles. Divers have also located the wreck of the 'Santa Maria de la Rosa', a vessel of Recalde's squadron, off the Blasket Islands, co. Kerry.

'Spanish Ships and Men sunk, drowned, and taken prisoner upon the coast of Ireland in September 1588.'

'At Loghfoile: ships, 1; men, 1,100. Sligo: ships, 3; men, 1,500. In Tiralie: ships, 1; men, 400. Cleere Island: ships, 1; men, 300. At Finglas in O'Mayle's country: ships, 1; men, 400. In

O'Flartie's country: ships, 1; men, 200. In Irris: ships, 2: the men saved in other vessels. In Galway haven one ship escaped, and lost prisoners, 70. In the river of Shenan, ships 1 burnt; the men saved in other ships.' Total of ships, 17; men, 5,394.

Signed: Geoffrey Fenton.

II. A Note of such Ships of the Spanish Fleet as perished in September 1588 upon the coast of Ireland, as are not in this former certificate.

One ship of 500 tons sunk in the Sound of Blaskie, near Dingle-Coushe; the men saved by Don Joan de Ricaldo, Admiral of the Biskayne fleet. A ship called the Barque of Hambroughe, of 600 tons, sunk by reason of a leak; 200 of her men saved by other ships. A Venetian ship, called La Valencera, wrecked in O'Doghertie's country. One ship wrecked in McSwynye ne Doe's country, near Loghsuylly; her men saved. A great ship wrecked in O'Boyle's country; the men saved. One ship wrecked near Dunluse, wherein about 300 men perished.

From *Calendar of Carew MSS 1575–88* (**19**), p. 472.

document 22
Rotten munitions and provisions

The supply of adequate provisions and munitions for the troops in Ireland was a constant problem. This was certainly a factor in making the Irish service unpopular with the troops.

PELHAM TO THE LORD TREASURER (BURLEIGH), FEBRUARY 1580

I was persuaded, when at Dublin, that her Majesty had nothing in staple here, but I have found so much that with £100 I have victualled *The Achates* for 10 weeks. And all this has been here until the beer is sour, the biscuit almost mouldy, and the beef old enough to be spent. I hear there is at Cork a great proportion of musty bread made at Dublin, and sent thither in the time of Sir William Drury's government.

From *Calendar of Carew MSS, 1575–88* (**18**), p. 220.

On the 19th I received of Henry Cripps, shipmaster, the last proportion of munition, but not altogether in the same nature as he did receive it by indenture with Sir Robert Constable. I received cannon corn-powder instead of fine corn-powder. The match and lead were very unequally proportioned, for the soldier is to have lead and match of other than equal weight to his powder. The 1,000 Handborough and Flanders corslets can never be issued to the garrison, as they are badly shaped and rotten. They were, as I think, of Sir Thomas Gressam's providing, and should be returned to the Tower. I also received 1,000 muskets complete, which are very excellent good, but not a morian, which is as great a want as we have any; neither to the 1,000 corslets either pike or halbert, which things we cannot be supplied of in this kingdom.

Not long since I sent one of my men to attend your Lordship and the rest of their Lordships for a supply of munitions.

From *Calendar of Carew MSS, 1589–1600* (**19**), pp. 24–5.

document 23

Battle of the Yellow Ford, 1598

This was the highest point of Tyrone's military achievement. The victory in the field over the English force was the fruit of some years of improved discipline and training. It was a distinct advance on Shane O'Neill's hit-and-run tactics, but nevertheless proved a flash in the pan, for O'Neil failed to gather the fruits of his victory, and was unable to sustain a campaign or win a battle outside Ulster, as the rout of Kinsale indicated.

'It was ordered that the army, setting forth in six regiments, should, if occasion required, join and make three bodies, and turn out their wings as they should see cause. Colonel Percye having the vanguard, the Marshal his second, should both join, and make one vanguard. Colonel Cosbie, having the vanguard of the battle, Sir Thomas Maria Winfeild his second, were appointed the like. Colonel Cunie, then Sergeant-Major, having the vanguard of the rear, Colonel Billings his second, were appointed the like.

'The Marshal, in respect that his regiment had the vanguard, would go there, notwithstanding that he was advised and persuaded by Sir T. M. Wingfeild to come in the battle and leave the vanguard to him. The like did Colonel Cunie, but neither could persuade him.

'The battle was commanded by Sir T. M. Wingfield, the rear by Colonel Cunie. The horse were divided into two bodies. The vanguard led by Sir Callistine Brooke, General of the horse; the point by Captain Mountgue, Lieutenant General; the rear by Captain Fleminge, marching betwixt the two rear regiments.

'The army thus marching, having bog and wood on either hand, within less than caliver shot, was fought withal within half a mile of Ardmaghe. The vanguard passed on over the ford, at the first bog, where the saker was left without stay until it came to the trench, and so forward. Cosie likewise passed the bog and left the saker. Sir T. M. Wingfield, coming thither, made there a stand, as well to carry off the saker as to attend the coming up of the rear regiments, whom he doubted to be greatly engaged, for that he heard them in great fight, and had no sight of them in long time before, by reason of a hill betwixt them. Of this he went to acquaint the Marshal, thinking to find the vanguard but a little before him, which could not then be seen by reason of the hill, purposing to have it to make good that place, and that himself would go with the battle to fetch off the rear, but it was so far off as the Marshal sent to them to make their retreat to that hill where he stood, and returned with Sir T. M. W. to the saker, which he then brought off by force of men, and went again with the Marshal, thinking that the vanguard had been come up, which was still advancing forward; and in all this time there was no sight of the rear. . . .

'Sir T. M. W., being come to his own regiment, saw the rear coming up, for whom he made a stand with his regiment at the boggy ford and went to tell the Marshal of their coming, in which time, he was slain; and the vanguard either having received message to make a retreat, or overlaid with the multitude of the enemy, wheeled about disorderly, which

advantage the enemy took, and brake them.' Captain Evans
was shot. Much of our powder took fire, wherewith many of
our men were slain and hurt. The Sergeant-Major and Captain
Montague then came to Wingfeild, and they determined to
retreat to Ardmaghe. Colonel Cosbie, however, without orders,
made an attack on the enemy. He was fetched off, 'broken as
the rest'.

Endorsed: '14 August 1598. The manner of the defeat given
to the Marshal at the Blackwater.'

From *Calendar of Carew MSS, 1589–1600* (**19**), pp. 280–1.

document 24
Mountjoy's methods of warfare

*The devastation of the countryside was a method of warfare practised by
the Gaelic lords in their internecine strife, and had been applied by Essex
in Ulster and by Pelham and others in the suppression of the Desmond
rebellion in Munster. Mountjoy, however, was the first to apply this form
of economic warfare systematically over a period of time. It was a ruthless
but efficient method of defeating an able and elusive enemy, and may be
compared in modern times to the methods used by the Crown forces to
defeat the communist guerrillas in the Malay jungle, 1948–60.*

The hearts of the English common souldiers broken with a
currant of disasterous successes, he heartned and incouraged, by
leading them warily, especially in his first actions, being more
carefull, that our men should not bee foiled, then that the rebels
should be attempted with boldnesse. To this end also, and that
he might bee ever at hand, as well to incourage and direct them
fighting, as to second them by any accident dismaied, he
bravely adventured his person, more then in the opinion of
Militarie wise men, a Generall should ordinarily hazard
himself (howsoever I must confesse, the nature of the Irish
fights, maintained upon passages, by sudden eruptions of
hidden rogues, doth more expose the Generall to these dangers,
then any other warre.)
My Lorde himselfe had his horse shot under him, his Gallo-
glasse carrying his helmet, had the same brused with the grasing

134

of a bullet upon it, yea, his Lordships very Grayhound, likewise using to waite at his stirrop, was shot through the body. Among his Lordships Chaplaines, Doctor Lattware was killed, and Mast. Ram had his horse shot under him. Among his Lordships Secretaries, Master Cranmer was killed, and my selfe had my thigh brused with a shot I received in my saddle.

The Rebels being swolne to the height of pride by their full numbers, and much more by continuall successe in their actions, hee proceeded in like sort with them, as formerly with his owne men, at the first warily tasting them with light skirmishes, yet he so prudently and bravely pursued his attempts, as he stil caried what he atempted.

The wise distribution of the forces availed him much: for first he planted Garrisons upon the chiefe rebels Countries, as likewise he compassed Tyrone on every side with them, which kept the rebels at home, so as they could not second one another, for feare of loosing their owne goods.

Againe, where other Deputies used to assaile the rebels onely in Summer time, this Lord prosecuted them most in the Winter, being commonly five daies at least in the weeke on horsebacke, all the Winter long. This brake their hearts; for the aire being sharpe, and they naked, and they being driven from their lodgings, into the Woods bare of leaves, they had no shelter for themselves. Besides that, their cattle (giving them no milke in the Winter) were also wasted by driving to and fro. Ad that they being thus troubled in the Seede time, could not sowe their ground. And as in Harvest time, both the Deputies forces, and the Garrisons, cut downe their Corne, before it was ripe, so now in Winter time they carried away, or burnt, all the stores of victuals in secret places, whether the Rebels had conveied them.

Againe, he had a speciall care to cut downe and cleare the difficult passages, that so our forces might with more safetie meete together, and upon all occasions second one another.

For protections and pardons (the easie obtaining whereof had formerly incouraged the rebels, aswell to enter into rebellion, as to breake their faith after submissions, in hope to be againe received to mercy), although it was necessary for the State in this generall rebellion, like a mother, to open her bosome to her children, lest being driven to dispaire, they should plunge themselves into all mischiefes, yet he never received any to mercy, but such as had so drawne bloud on their fellow rebels, and were themselves made so poore, as there was small danger of their relaps. To which ende he forbad al conferences and parleys with the rebels, by pretence whereof many treacherous plots had formerly beene drawne, by the false-hearted subjects, and many corruptions had been practised by some covetous commanders. But to such as were received to mercy, (that he might take away the diffidence they had long conceived of the State), he kept his word inviolable.

From Fynes Moryson, *Itinerary* (**28**), ii, 268–71.

V. PLANTATION SCHEMES

document 25
Letter of the Earl of Surrey to Henry VIII, 1521

Surrey regarded Henry VIII's policy of 'sober ways, politic drifts and amiable persuasions' as unrealistic, and put forward instead his case for military conquest and subsequent plantation of English colonies among the 'mere' Irish.

After my poor opinion, this land shall never be brought to good order and due subjection, but only by conquest; which is, at your Grace's pleasure, to be brought to pass two manner of ways. One way is, if your Grace will one year set on hand to win one country, and another year, another country, and so continue, till all at length be won. After my opinion, the least number that your Grace must occupy, can be no less than 2,500; ...

And if your Grace will, in more brief time, have your purpose brought to pass, and to set upon the conquest in divers places, at one time; then, after my poor opinion, 6,000 men is the least number that your Grace must occupy. . . .

Also, if it shall like your Grace to set on hand with the said conquest, your Grace must furnish the most part of the number with victuals, and carriage for the same, out of England, or some other countries; for here is much to do, to furnish this company that is now here. And ever, as the countries shall fortune to be won, strong towns and fortresses must be builded upon the same.

And after my poor opinion, unless your Grace send inhabitants, of your own natural subjects, to inhabit such countries as shall be won, all your charges should be but wastefully spent. For if this country's people, of the Irish, should inhabit, undoubtedly they would return to their old ill-rooted customs ... according as they have ever yet done, and daily do.

From S.P. Hen. VIII, ii. 73–5, printed in (**17**), pp. 89–91.

document 26

Memoranda by Sir Francis Knollys, 1567

This document provided some suggestions about the settlement of Ulster after the death of Shane O'Neill. Humphrey Gilbert was named as a suitable president of Ulster whose job it would be to balance Turlough O'Neill and the MacDonnells of Antrim, and to encourage a colony of English farmers and artisans to establish themselves in the province.

7 JULY 1567. MEMORANDA BY SIR FRANCIS KNOLLYS

Yf Turlough Lynoghe shall styll kleame to be Oneale rebellyously, than to offer elyxander ogge, with the newe Skottes, his free holde for theyr habitation, yf theye entryng forthwith theruppon shall expell hym & keape the same.

And yff Turlough be a good subject than to expell the skotts forthwith

To gyve no cowntenance of honor to Turloghe, otherwyse than that he may be governed as mr Ager dothe governe the Bernes & Toolles, untyll a president & cownsayle be establisshed there.

That mr gylbard be made president there for the first yere or two, yff he joynyng with his frendes of ye weste woll plant habitation there of ynglyshe men with resonable conditions.

To provoke sotche of ye thowsand men that are to be cassed beyng good husbond men, plowe wryghts, kart wryghts, and Smythes, eyther to take habitation yf they be hable, or els to staye & serve there under sotche gentlemen as shall inhabyte there.

And as soone as may be to cawse artizans, and sea fysshers to plant uppon the Ban; at Strangford, and at Lowghfoyle, intrenchyng theym selffes there, that after they may growe to be haven Townes.

From *The Voyages and Colonising Enterprises of Sir Humphrey Gilbert* (**67**), i, 121.

document 27

Proposal for a colony in Munster

Just as the Spaniards hastened to exploit the people and resources of the New World, so the West Country adventurers sought to exploit the potential wealth of Ireland. Munster, with its towns and fisheries, open to Spanish influence and bedevilled by internal strife, appeared an obvious proving ground for colonial development. Gilbert and his associates sought to form a chartered corporation with monopolistic privileges. Such organisations were destined to play an important role in the expansion of English trade and in the early history of the American colonies.

A note of Sutch demaundes as Certeyne gentlemen mynde to be Sutours to the Queenes moste excellent majesty for the Fisshing of the South and Southwest Seas of Ireland and enjoying of sutch havens Ilandes and Castells as hereafter Followeth.

Furste. To have of her highness in fee fearme, the havens of Balletemoore, and Beere haven, with the Ilandes of Cape cleer, Inyskircan and the other Ilandes with in the haven of Balletemoore, and the Ilandes belonging to beere haven, with all sutch landes spirituall and temporall as apperteine unto those Ilandes. And also to have the comodity of the other Ilandes and havens, which are in her highnes gifte, from the Towne of Rosse to the sounde of Blaskey / And also to have lysence of her majesty to fortiffye and build upon the maine land of those havens.

Item to have a graunte from her majesty, to make a Corporat Towne, and to fortiffy the same at the haven of Balletemoore, And also at Beere haven, or upon eny of the Ilandes aforesaid, as shall seeme best to the discrecion of the gentlemen of that

138

corporacion uppon their arrivall there, as they like to build or inhabit.

Item to have from her highnes full Aucthority to excecute in the Same Towne the Lawes of this Realme in all matteres / Savinge in Cases of highe Threason, in as lardge and Ample manner, as has eny other Coporat Towne in Ireland.

Item the seid corporacion, to have graunte from her majesty to make Sutch statutes and lawes as shall seeme good to their discrecions, for the better ordring of them selves, and their people, those being agreeable to the lawes of this Realme.

Item to have lysence from her highnes to have the traffick of the same partes of the Country, in as lardge and ample manner, as the other Corporat. Townes have, in the Sowth and South-west of Ireland.

Items to have lysence of her majesty to traffick & trade with their marchandice, into alle partes of christendom excepting sutch places as are by former grauntes from her highnes prohibitted, or Contrary to the Lawes of the Realme of Ireland.

Item in Consideracion that the same enterprise will be a greate Chardge to the gentlemen, And that the quenes hignes shall have the yerely rent of Two hundreth poundes Currant money of England to her and her heires for ever, after three yeres, They therefore desire to have graunte from her majesty to have free Course and recourse with their marchandice / withowt paying eny maner of Custome more then the yerely rent

Item to have Comission from her majesty to take uppe Fower hundred men of Sutch Occupacons as shall serve that turne, to be employed about the defence and fortiffying of those havens and Ilandes and keeping of them. The chardges of which men to be disbursed by the gentlemen of that Corporacion.

Item to have of her highnes in gift, towardes their first begin-yng of their fortifficacons and maintennaunce of a Gally and Briggenden Two hundred Condempned men of the Realme of Ireland to be imployed as the gentlemen of the Corporacion shall thinke good

In consideracion of the graunte of the Premisses the said gentlemen are agreed to yelde unto her majesty her heirs & Successours, A yerely rent of Two hundred poundes Current monney of England after three yeres / And so for Somany yeres as the said Townes or fortes shalbe by the gentlemen, their heires executors or assynes maineteyned

> Sir Warrham Sentleger
> Mr Edward Sentlowe
> Mr Grenfeld
> Mr Thomas Leton
> Mr Umfrey Gilbert
> Mr Jaques Wyngfeld
> Mr Gilbart Talbott

From *The Voyages and Colonising Enterprises of Sir Humphrey Gilbert* (**67**), i, 122–4.

document 28

Spenser's views of Ireland

Spenser came to Ireland in 1580 as secretary to the Lord Deputy, Lord Grey de Wilton. He acquired property, achieved office as Registrar of Chancery, and settled at Kilcoman castle, co. Cork, in 1588. He later was present at the massacre of Smerwick, and witnessed the miseries of warfare in Munster. Yet, he had a poet's eye for the beauties of the Irish landscape and saw its potential richness. Kilcolman was burnt in the Munster rising of 1598. Spenser fled to London, where he died in the following year.

Sure it is . . . a most beautiful and sweet country as any is under heaven: seamed throughout with many goodly rivers, replenished with all sorts of fish, most abundantly sprinkled with many sweet islands and goodly lakes, like little inland seas, that will carry even ships upon their waters, adorned with goodly woods fit for building of houses and ships, so commodiously, as that if some princes in the world had them, they would soon hope to be lords of all the seas, and ere long of all the world: also full of good ports and havens opening upon England and Scotland, as inviting us to come to them, to see what excellent commodities that country can afford, besides the soil itself is most fertile, fit to yield all kinds of fruit that shall be committd thereunto. And lastly, the heavens most mild and temperate, though somewhat more moist than the part towards the west.

. . .

For, notwithstanding that [Munster] was a most rich and plentiful country, full of corn and cattle, that you would have thought they should have been able to stand long, yet ere one year and a half they were brought to such wretchedness as that any stony heart would have rued the same. Out of every corner of the woods and glens they came creeping forth upon their hands, for their legs could not bear them; they looked like anatomies of death; they spake like ghosts crying out of their graves; they did eat the dead carrions, happy where they could find them; yea, and one another soon after, insomuch as the very carcasses they spared not to scrape out of their graves; and if they found a plot of watercresses or shamrocks, there they flocked as to a feast for the time, yet not able long to continue there withal; that in short space there were none almost left, and a most populous and plentiful country suddenly left void of man and beast; yet, sure, in all that war there perished not many by the sword, but all by the extremity of famine which they themselves had wrought.

From Edmund Spenser, *A View of the State of Ireland* (**21**), pp. 54, 143-4.

document 29

Estimate of the cost charges of plantation in Munster, 1585

To induce people to settle in Munster this estimate of their costs during the first year was prepared. Such a detailed assessment of the cost of living was designed to induce Londoners, Bristolians and younger sons to cross St George's Channel to win instant fortune.

The Gentleman's charge.—6 hinds, at 53*s*. 4*d*. each; 4 women, at 33*s*. 4*d*. each; 2 boys, ditto; 12 quarters of wheat or rye, at 26*s*. 8*d*.; 12 qrs. barley, at 13*s*. 4*d*.; weekly victuals, besides butter and cheese of their own making, 6*s*. 8*d*. Stock: 25 kine, at 1*l*. 6*s*. 8*d*. each; 100 yearlings, at 12*s*. each; 8 oxen, at 50*s*. each; 4 garrons, at 25*s*. each; 300 ewes, at 4*s*. each. For sowing: 10 qrs. wheat and rye, 11 qrs. barley, 5 qrs. beans, at 13*s*. 4*d*.

each; 20 qrs. oats, at 9s. Sum total, 278l.; whereof there will be spent this year 67l. 6s. 8d.; and the remainder in stock to increase.

The Farmer's charge.—2 hinds, at 53s. 4d.; one boy and a maid-servant, at 26s. 8d.; 5 qrs. wheat or rye for bread; 6 qrs. oats for drink; weekly victuals, besides butter and cheese of their own making, 3s. 4d. Stock: 4 oxen, a garron, 10 kine, 10 heifers' yearlings, two others, 30 ewes. For sowing: of wheat and rye, 2 qrs.; of barley, 2; beans, 1; oats, 4. Total 70l. 7s.; whereof to be spent this year 26l. 0s. 8d.; the rest to remain in stock.

Copyholders.—One hind, 40s.; one maid-servant, 26s. 8d.; 4 qrs. wheat and rye for diet, 4 qrs. of oats for drink; weekly victuals, 20d.; 5 kine; 2 yearling steers, 25s. the two; 10 ewes, at 3s. 4d. each. For sowing: 2 qrs. wheat and rye, 1 qr. barley, beans, and oats. Total, 28l. 16s. 8d.; whereof to be spent this year 14l. 16s.; the remainder in stock.

Cottagers.—2 qrs. wheat or rye; 2 qrs. oats for drink; 2 kine. Total, 6l. 4s. 8d.; whereof to be spent this year 71s. 4d.; the rest in stock.

From *Calendar of Carew MSS, 1575–88* (**19**), p. 413.

document 30

Foundation of the University of Dublin

It was not until the reign of Elizabeth that serious consideration began to be given to the establishment of a University in Ireland. Sir James Stanihurst, the Recorder of Dublin, and, later, Sir John Perrot, made proposals for a University in Dublin, but they were not successful. However, in 1592 the Mayor and Corporation of Dublin granted the lands of the dissolved abbey of All Hallows to the proposed institution, and the Queen gave the foundation charter. The University was founded for the increase of 'knowledge and Civility' in the Kingdom, to provide an alternative to foreign universities and to support the ecclesiastical settlement. The original intention that Trinity College would be the first of several, on the pattern of Oxford or Cambridge, was never realised, although degrees granted by the University of Dublin are still recognised ad eundem gradum by those universities.

That there shall be one College the mother of a University in a certain place called All Hallows near Dublin, for the education, institution, and instruction of youth and students in Arts and Faculties, to continue for ever; and which will be called the College of the Holy and Undivided Trinity near Dublin founded by the most Serene Queen Elizabeth. That College [to consist] of one Provost, and of three Fellows in the name of more, and three Scholars in the name of more. The Provost, Fellows, and Scholars of the aforesaid Trinity College, and their successors in deed, fact, and name. . shall be one body corporate and politic, for ever incorporated and erected by the name of the Provost, Fellows, and Scholars of the College of the Holy Trinity . . . near Dublin.

From *Chartae Collegii Sanctae et Individuae Trinitatis* (Dublin 1879), pp. 1–3.

We, Thomas Smith, Mayor of Dublin, George Kennedy and John Mills, Sheriffs of the same city, the Commonalty and Citizens of the city, have given to the Provost, Fellows, and Scholars of the College, the whole house of All Hallows and churchyard thereof, also all gardens, grounds, pastures, . . . which extend from Hoggen-green [College Green] to the lands of the late Abbey of the Virgin on the East; and from the lane which leads to the fountain of St. Patrick on the South to the river Liffey on the North. They and all the students devoted to literature may be freed from all taxes of the city. . In witness whereof we have affixed our common seal, and the Provost, Fellows, and Scholars have affixed their common seal. Dublin, July 21st, 1592.

From W. Urwick, *Early History of Trinity College Dublin*, p. 9.

The Flight of the Earls   **document 31**

In 1607 Hugh O'Neill, Earl of Tyrone, and his ally, the Earl of Tyrconnell, sailed into voluntary exile from Rathmullan. This action may be compared with the flight of Prince Charles Edward Stuart after

143

the Jacobite defeat at Culloden, for in both cases there was a romantic and symbolic ending of a Gaelic order. This 'Flight of the Earls', coinciding as it did with the foundation of Jamestown in Virginia, cleared the way for the plantation of Ulster. Significantly, as in the case of the exiled Stuarts, no continental power was willing to afford effective help for the restoration of the earls to their lost heritage.

It is true that they are embarked and gone with the most part of that company of men, women and children, who are named in the proclamation: it is true they took shipping the 14th of this present September; that the Saturday before the Earl of Tyrone was with my Lord Deputy at Slane ... that from thence he went to Mellifont, Sir Garret Moore's house, where he wept abundantly when he took his leave, giving a solemn farewell to every child and every servant in the house, which made them all marvel, because it was not his manner to use such compliments. From thence, on Sunday, he went to Dundalk; on Monday he went to Dungannon, where he rested two whole days; on Wednesday night, they say, he travelled all night with his impediments, that is, his women and children; and it is likewise reported that the Countess, his wife, being exceedingly weary, slipped down from her horse, and, weeping, said she could go no farther; whereupon the Earl drew his sword, and swore a great oath that he would kill her in the place, if she would not pass on with him, and put on a more cheerful countenance withal. Yet, the next day, when he came near Lough Foyle, his passage that way was not so secret but the Governor there had notice thereof, and invited him and his son to dinner; but their haste was such that they accepted not that courtesy, but they went on, and came that Thursday night to Rathmullan, a town on the west side of Lough Swilly, where the Earl of Tyrconnel and his company met him. . . .

It is certain that Tyrone, in his heart, repines at the English government in his country, where, until his last submission, as well before his rebellion as in the time of his rebellion, he ever lived like a free prince, or rather like an absolute tyrant there. But now the law of England, and the ministers thereof, were shackles and handlocks unto him, and the garrisons planted in his country were as pricks in his side; besides, to evict any part of that land from him, which he has hitherto held after the Irish manner, making all the tenants thereof his villeins . . . this was as grievous unto him as to pinch away the quick flesh from his body.

From *Calendar of State Papers Ireland 1606–8* (**18**), pp. 270–4.

The Plantation in Ulster

document 32

These two extracts show the realistic approach to the problems of colonisation in the early seventeenth century. They form a contrast to the theorising of Sir Thomas Smith, and the entrepreneurial outlook of Sir Humphrey Gilbert and his associates a generation earlier.

Planting of countries is like planting of woods; for you must make account to leese almost twenty years' profit, and expect your recompense in the end. For the principal thing that hath been the destruction of most plantations, hath been the base and hasty drawing of profit in the first years. The people wherewith you plant ought to be gardeners, ploughmen, labourers, smiths, carpenters, joiners, fishermen, fowlers, with some few apothecaries, surgeons, cooks, and bakers. In a country of plantation, first look about, what kind of victual the country yields of itself to hand; as chestnuts, walnuts, pine-apples, olives, dates, plums, cherries, wild honey, and the like; and make use of them. Then consider what victual or esculent things there are, which grow speedily, and within the year; as parsnips, carrots, turnips, onions, radish, artichokes of Hierusalem, maize, and the like. For wheat, barley, and oats, they ask too much labour; but with peas and beans you may begin, both because they ask less labour, and because they serve for meat as well as for bread. And of rice likewise cometh a great increase, and it is a kind of meat. Above all, there ought to be brought store of biscuit, oat-meal, flour, meal, and the like, in the beginning, till bread may be had. For beasts or birds, take chiefly such as are least subject to diseases, and multiply fastest; as swine, goats, cocks, hens, turkeys, geese, house-doves, and the like. Consider likewise what commodities the soil where the plantation is doth naturally yield, that they may some way help to defray the charge of the plantation: so it be not, as was said, to the untimely prejudice of the main business; as it hath fared with tobacco in Virginia.

From Francis Bacon, *Essay III, 'Of Plantations'* (**22**).

That the woods, grounds and soil of Glenconkein and Killitragh . . . be wholly to the City in perpetuity, the timber trees of those woods to be converted to the use of the plantation, and all necessary uses in Ireland, and not to be made merchandise. . . .

That the City shall have the patronage of all the churches as well within the city of Derry and town of Coleraine as in all lands undertaken by them.

That the 4,000 acres laid to the city of Derry and town of Coleraine shall be in fee farm at the yearly rent of 5*s*. 4*d*.

That the city of Derry and county of Coleraine and 7,000 acres of land to them, shall be held of the King in free burgage.

That no flax, hemp or yarn, unwoven, be carried out of the Derry and Coleraine without license of the City's officers, and that no hides be transferred without like license. . . .

That sufficient forces shall be maintained at the King's charge for the undertakers' safety for a certain time. . . .

That the City shall with all speed set forward the plantation in such sort that there may be 60 houses built in Derry and 40 in Coleraine by the 1st November following, with convenient fortifications, the rest of the houses to be built and perfected by 1st November 1611.

From *Contemporary Sources 1509–1610* (**17**), pp. 289–90.

Bibliography

GENERAL

1 Beckett, J. C. *A Short History of Ireland*, Hutchinson University Library, 3rd edn, 1966.
2 Moody, T. W. and Martin, F. X., eds. *The Course of Irish History*, Cork, Mercier Press, 1967.
3 Curtis, E. *A History of Ireland*, 6th edn, Methuen, 1960.
4 Hull, Eleanor. *A History of Ireland and her People to the Close of the Tudor Period*, Harrap, 1926.
5 Otway-Ruthven, Annette Jocelyn. *A History of Medieval Ireland*, Benn, 1968.
6 Bagwell, R. *Ireland under the Tudors*, Longmans, 1885–90 (reprinted 1963), 3 vols: the standard general work on the period.
7 Bindoff, S. T. *Tudor England*, Penguin Books (Pelican), 1950.
8 Black, J. B. *The Reign of Elizabeth*, Oxford University Press, 1936.
9 Woodward, G. W. O. *Reformation and Resurgence, 1485–1603*, Longmans, 1963; contains a perceptive section on Ireland.
10 Rowse, A. L. *The Expansion of Elizabethan England*, Macmillan, 1955: indicates the strain placed upon England's resources by Tyrone's war, 1594–1603.
11 Bagwell, R. *Ireland Under the Stuarts*, Longmans, 1909–16, 3 vols.
12 Beckett, J. C. *The Making of Modern Ireland, 1603–1923*, Faber, 1966.
13 Freeman, T. W. *Ireland: its physical, historical, social and economic geography*, Methuen, 1950.
14 Evans, E. E. *Irish Folkways*, Routledge and Kegan Paul, 1957.
15 Cullen, L. M. *Life in Ireland*, Batsford, 1968.

16 Curtis, E. and McDowell, R. B., eds. *Irish Historical Documents 1172–1922*, Methuen, 1943: mainly of political and constitutional interest.

17 Maxwell, Constantia, *Irish History from Contemporary Sources, 1509–1610*, Allen & Unwin, 1923: has a useful introductory section, and is especially good for social and economic history.

18 Hamilton, H. C., ed., and others. *Calendar of State Papers, Ireland*, Longmans, 1867–1910, 13 vols: an invaluable collection of printed source material, though somewhat weak for the period 1547–85; fuller for the years 1586–1603.

19 Brewer, J. S. and Bullen, W., eds. *Calendar of the Carew Manuscripts preserved in the Archepiscopal Library at Lambeth*, Longmans, 1870–3: papers collected and annotated by Sir George Carew and bequeathed to his nephew Thomas Stafford, who sold the MSS to Archbishop Laud.

20 Stafford, T. *Pacata Hibernia; or a history of the wars in Ireland during the reign of Elizabeth*, London, 1633: based on the correspondence of Sir George Carew and Thomas Stafford's own experience as an officer in Munster; deals particularly with the campaigns in the south of Ireland, the battle of Kinsale, and the final defeat of Hugh O'Neill.

21 Morley, H., ed. *Ireland under Elizabeth and James the First*, Routledge, 1890: contains descriptions of Ireland by Edmund Spenser, Sir John Davies and Fynes Moryson.

22 Freeman, A. M. ed. *The Compossicion Booke of Conought*, Dublin, Stationery Office, 1936; with index prepared by G. A. Hayes-McCoy, 1942.

23 Spedding, J., and others, eds. *The works of Francis Bacon*, Longmans, 1857–9.

24 Davies, Sir J. *A Discoverie of the True Causes why Ireland was Never Entirely Subdued*, John Jaggard, 1613.

25 Grosart, A. B., ed. *The Lismore Papers*, privately printed, 1886–8, 10 vols: being the letters and diaries of Richard Boyle, first earl of Cork.

26 Rawlinson, R., ed. *The History of Sir John Perrott*, London, 1728: an edition of the original MS written towards the close of Elizabeth's reign.

27 Laughton, J. K., ed. *State Papers Relating to the Defeat of the Spanish Armada*, 2nd edn, Navy Records Society, 1895, 2 vols.

28 Moryson, Fynes. *An Itinerary, Containing his Ten Yeares Travell through Germany . . . Switzerland . . . Poland . . . England, Scotland, Ireland,* Glasgow, James MacLehose, 1907–8, 4 vols: reprinted in full for the first time since the original publication by John Beale of Aldersgate Street, 1617.

29 O'Donovan, J., ed. *Annals of the kingdom of Ireland by the Four Masters,* Hodges and Smith (Dublin), 1848, 5 vols: these annals were compiled in the early seventeenth century by Michael O'Clery, Conary O'Clery, Lughaidh O'Clery and Ferfeasa O'Mulcoury.

30 O'Cianan, Tadhg. *The Flight of the Earls,* ed. Rev. P. Walsh, Dublin, M. H. Gill and Son, 1916.

31 O'Clery, L., *The Life of Hugh Roe O'Donnell,* ed. Rev. D. Murphy, Dublin, Sealey, Bryen and Walker, 1893.

ECONOMIC AND SOCIAL HISTORY

32 Chart, D. A. *Economic History of Ireland,* Dublin, Talbot Press, 1920.

33 Longfield, A. K. *Anglo-Irish Trade in the Sixteenth Century,* Routledge, 1929.

34 Butler, W. F. T. *Confiscation in Irish History,* 2nd edn, Dublin, Talbot Press, 1918.

35 Falkiner, C. L. *Illustrations of Irish History and Topography,* Longmans, 1904: prints the substance of Fynes Moryson's and Sir Josias Bodley's observations of their Irish travels.

36 Falkiner, C. L. *Essays Relating to Ireland,* Longmans, 1909: deals with such topics as Spenser in Ireland, Sir John Davies, and the towns of Galway and Youghal.

37 Chart, D. A. *The Story of Dublin,* Dent, 1907.

38 Gilbert, Sir J. T. *A History of the City of Dublin,* Dublin, McGlashan, 1854–9.

39 O'Sullivan, W. *Economic History of Cork City,* Cork University Press, 1937.

40 O'Sullivan, Mary D. *Old Galway,* Heffer, 1942.

41 Hardiman, J. *The History of Galway,* Dublin, 1820, reprinted by the 'Connacht Tribune', Galway, 1926.

42 O'Flaherty, R. *A Chorographical Description of West or H-iar Connaught,* ed. J. Hardiman, University Press (Dublin), 1846: a fully annotated edition of the late seventeenth-century text.

43   Knox, H. T. *The History of Mayo*, Hodges, Figgis (Dublin), 1908.

44   Hutchison, W. R. *Tyrone Precinct*, Belfast, Mayne, 1951: provides much detail of the local history of the Dungannon area.

45   McSkimin, S. *The History and Antiquities of Carrickfergus*, ed. E. J. McCrum, Belfast, Mullan, 1909.

46   Benn, G. *A History of the Town of Belfast*, Marcus Ward, 1877–1880.

47   Maxwell, Constantia. *A History of Trinity College, Dublin*, Dublin University Press, 1946.

ECCLESIASTICAL

48   Phillips, W. A., ed. *History of the Church of Ireland*, Oxford University Press, 1933–4, 3 vols.

49   Reid, J. S. *History of the Presbyterian Church in Ireland*, 3rd edn by W. D. Killen, Belfast, Mullan, 1867.

50   Edwards, R. D. *Church and State in Tudor Ireland*, Dublin, Talbot Press, 1935.

51   Ronan, M. V. *The Reformation in Ireland under Elizabeth, 1558–80*, Longmans, 1930.

52   Bindoff, S. T., Hurstfield, J. and Williams, C. H., eds. *Elizabethan Government and Society*, Athlone Press, 1961: contains a contribution by R. D. Edwards on 'Ireland, Elizabeth and the counter-reformation', pp. 315–39.

ANGLO-IRISH AND NATIVE LORDSHIP

53   Conway, Agnes. *Henry VII's Relations with Scotland and Ireland 1485–98*, Cambridge University Press, 1932.

54   Bryan, D. *Gerald Fitzgerald, the Great Earl of Kildare (1456–1513)*, Dublin, Talbot Press, 1933.

55   Fitzgerald, B. *The Geraldines, an Experiment in Irish Government, 1169–1601*, Staples Press, 1951: contains a useful survey of the Geraldines in the sixteenth century.

56   Butler, W. F. T. *Gleanings from Irish history*, Longmans, 1925: contains sections on the policy of surrender and regrant, and the MacCarthy chiefries in west Cork.

57   O'Faolain, S. *The great O'Neill*, Longmans, 1942: a popular though somewhat dated account of Hugh O'Neill.

58   Lee, G. A. 'The White Knights and their kinsmen', in *North*

Munster Studies, ed. E. Rynne, 251–65, Limerick, Thomond Archaeological Society, 1967.

59 Hill, G. *An Historical Account of the MacDonnells of Antrim*, Belfast, Archer, 1873.

60 Hogan, J. 'Shane O'Neill comes to the court of Elizabeth', in *Essays and studies presented to Professor Tadhg Ua Donnchadha*, ed. S. Pender, Cork University Press, 1947.

61 Hayes-McCoy, G. A. 'Gaelic society in Ireland in the late sixteenth century', in *Historical Studies IV*, ed. G. A. Hayes-McCoy, Bowes, 1963.

IRELAND AND THE NEW WORLD

62 Quinn, D. B. *The Elizabethans and the Irish*, Cornell University Press, 1966: published for the Folger Shakespeare Library.

63 Rowse, A. L. *The Elizabethans and America*, Macmillan, 1959.

64 Dewar, Mary. *Sir Thomas Smith*, Oxford University Press, 1964: a valuable modern study of a forgotten scholar/statesman.

65 Strype, J. *Life of the learned Sir Thomas Smith Kt*, London, 1698 (reprinted 1820).

66 Quinn, D. B. *Raleigh and the British Empire*, English Universities Press, 1947.

67 Quinn, D. B. ed. *The voyages and colonising enterprises of Sir Humphrey Gilbert*, Hakluyt Society, 1940, 2 vols.

68 Quinn, D. B., ed. *The Roanoke Voyages, 1584–90*, Hakluyt Society, 1955, 2 vols: documents Sir Walter Raleigh's interests in both Munster and Virginia.

69 Williams, N. L. *Sir Walter Raleigh*, Eyre & Spottiswoode, 1962; Penguin, 1965.

70 Judson, A. C. *Notes on the Life of Edmund Spenser*, Indiana University Press, 1949.

71 Devereux, W. B. *Lives and Letters of the Devereux Earls of Essex*, John Murray, 1853, 2 vols.

MILITARY HISTORY

72 Leask, H. G. *Irish Castles and Castellated Houses*, Dundalk, Dundalgan Press, 1941.

73 Cruickshank, G. B. *Elizabeth's Army*, 2nd edn, Oxford University

Press, 1966: deals with the problems of military organization in this period.

74 Falls, C. *Elizabeth's Irish Wars*, Methuen, 1950: a sound and readable account, which has provided the basis for further research.

75 Hayes-McCoy, G. A. *Scots Mercenary Forces in Ireland*, Dublin, Burns Oates & Washbourne, 1937: a lucid investigation into a significant aspect of sixteenth-century history.

76 Hayes-McCoy, G. A., ed. *The Irish at War*, Cork, Mercier Press, 1964: contains a contribution by C. Falls on 'The battle of the Yellow Ford'.

77 Allingham, H. *Captain Cuellar's Adventures in Connacht and Ulster*, with *Captain Cuellar's Narrative of the Spanish Armada and his adventures in Ireland*, trans. by R. Crawford, Elliot Stock, 1897.

78 Hardy, E. *Survivors of the Armada*, Constable, 1966: contains a new translation of Cuellar's narrative with detailed commentary.

79 Hayes-McCoy, G. A. *Irish Battles*, Longman, 1969: a military history with chapters on Farsetmore, Clontibret, The Yellow Ford, Moyry Pass and Kinsale.

80 Hayes-McCoy, G. A. *Ulster and other Irish maps, c. 1600*, Dublin, Stationery Office, 1964: facsimile reproductions of contemporary maps by Richard Bartlett together with explanatory notes by the author.

81 Falls, C. *Mountjoy: Elizabethan General*, Odhams Press, 1955.

82 Jones, F. M. *Mountjoy, 1563–1606: the last Elizabethan Deputy*, Dublin, Clonmore and Reynolds, 1958.

IRELAND AND EUROPE

83 Mattingly, G. *The Defeat of the Spanish Armada*, Cape, 1959: Penguin (Pelican), 1962.

84 Petrie, Sir Charles, *Philip II of Spain*, Eyre & Spottiswoode, 1963.

85 Silke, J. J., *Ireland and Europe 1559–1607*, Dundalk, Dundalgan Press, 1966.

THE JACOBEAN PLANTATION

86 Moody, T. W. *The Londonderry Plantation, 1609–41*, Belfast, Mullan, 1939: the definitive modern work on this aspect of the Ulster plantation.

87 Stevenson, J. *Two Centuries of Life in Down, 1600–1800*, Belfast, McCaw, Stevenson and Orr, 1920.

88 Hill, G. *An Historical Account of the Plantation in Ulster at the Commencement of the Seventeenth Century, 1608–20*, Belfast, McCaw, Stevenson and Orr, 1877.

89 Bigger, F. J. *Sir Arthur Chichester, Lord Deputy of Ireland*, Belfast, 1904.

90 Chart, D. A., ed. *Londonderry and the London Companies 1609–29*, Belfast, H.M.S.O., 1928: letters and papers of Sir Thomas Phillips, illustrated by reproductions of contemporary prints.

91 Hill, G., ed. *The Montgomery Manuscripts (1603–1706)*, Belfast, Cleeland, 1869.

ARTICLES

92 Addyman, P. 'Coney Island, Lough Neagh: prehistoric settlement, Anglo-Norman castle and Elizabethan native fortress', *Ulster Journal of Archaeology*, 3rd series, xxviii (1965), 78–101.

93 Butler, G. 'The battle of Affane', *Irish Sword*, viii (1967), 33–46.

94 Danaher, K. 'Armada losses on the Irish Coast', *Irish Sword*, ii (1956), 321–31.

95 Edwards, R. D. and Moody, T. W. 'The history of Poynings' Law 1494–1615', *Irish Historical Studies*, ii (1941), 415–24.

96 Falls, C. 'Niall Garve O'Donnell', *Irish Sword*, i (1949–50), 2–7.

97 Falls, C. 'Mountjoy as a soldier', *Irish Sword*, ii. (1954), 1–5.

98 Falls, C. 'The growth of Irish military strength in the second half of the sixteenth century', *Irish Sword*, ii (1955), 103–6.

99 Green, W. S. 'The wrecks of the Spanish Armada on the coast of Ireland', *Geographical Journal*, xxxvii (1906), 429–51.

100 Hayes-McCoy, G. A. 'Strategy and tactics in Irish warfare, 1593–1601', *Irish Historical Studies*, ii (1941), 255–79.

101 Hayes-McCoy, G. A. 'The tide of victory and defeat: I. The battle of Clontibret, 1595; II. The battle of Kinsale, 1601', *Studies*, xxxviii (1949), 158–86, 307–17.

102 Hayes-McCoy, G. A. 'The army of Ulster, 1593–1601', *Irish Sword*, i (1950–1), 15–17.

103 Henry, L. W. 'Contemporary sources for Essex's lieutenancy in Ireland, 1599', *Irish Historical Studies*, xi (1958–59), 8–17.

104 Jones, F. M. 'The Spaniards and Kinsale 1601', *Journal of the Galway Historical and Archaeological Society*, xxi (1944), 1–43.

105 Jones, F. M. 'An indictment of Don Juan del Aguila', *Irish Sword*, ii (1955), 217–20.

106 McCracken, Eileen. 'The woodlands of Ireland c. 1600', *Irish Historical Studies*, xi (1959), 271–96.

107 Mangan, H. 'A vindication of Don Juan del Aguila', *Irish Sword*, ii (1956), 342–51.

108 Moody, T. W. 'The Irish parliament under Elizabeth and James I', *Proceedings of the Royal Irish Academy*, xlv C 6 (1939), 41–81.

109 Morton, R. G. 'The enterprise of Ulster', *History Today*, xvii (1967), 114–21.

110 Morton, R. G. 'Naval activity on Lough Neagh 1558–1603', *Irish Sword*, viii (1969).

111 O'Domhnaill, S. 'Warfare in sixteenth century Ireland', *Irish Historical Studies*, v (1946), 29–54.

112 O'Malley, Sir Owen. 'Note on the O'Malley lordship at the close of the sixteenth century', *Journal of the Galway Historical and Archaeological Society*, xxiv (1950), 27–57.

113 Pollen, J. H. 'The Irish expedition of 1579', *The Month*, C i (1903), 69–85: provides details of Thomas Stukeley's enterprise.

114 Quinn, D. B. ' "A discourse of Ireland" (circa 1599): a sidelight on English colonial policy', *Proceedings of the Royal Irish Academy*, xlvii C 3 (1942), 151–66.

115 Quinn, D. B. 'Sir Thomas Smith (1513–1577) and the beginnings of English colonial theory', *Proceedings of the American Philosophical Society*, lxxxix (1945), 543–60.

116 Quinn, D. B. 'Agenda for Irish history: II. Ireland from 1461 to 1603', *Irish Historical Studies*, iv (1945), 258–69.

117 Quinn, D. B. 'Henry VIII and Ireland, 1509–34', *Irish Historical Studies*, xii (1961), 318–44.

118 Ranger, T. O. 'Richard Boyle and the making of an Irish fortune, 1585–1614', *Irish Historical Studies*, x (1957), 257–97.

119 Silke, J. J. 'Why Aguila landed at Kinsale', *Irish Historical Studies*, xiii (1963), 236–45.

120 Silke, J. J. 'Spain and the invasion of Ireland, 1601–2', *Irish Historical Studies*, xiv (1965), 295–312.

121 White, D. G. 'The reign of Edward VI in Ireland: some political, social and economic aspects', *Irish Historical Studies*, xiv (1965), 197–211.: deals with the inception of the policy of plantation.

122 Walsh, Micheline, 'The last years of Hugh O'Neill', *Irish Sword*, iii (1957–8), *et seq.*
123 Walsh, P. 'Historical criticism of the life of Hugh Roe O'Donnell', *Irish Historical Studies*, i (1939), 229–50.

Index

Index

Clandeboy, 36, 37, 41, 79, 88

Clanrickard, 12, 18, 61, 62, 70

Clare (Thomond), 50, 65, 66, 74

Clare island, 74, 75

Clew bay, 66, 74

Clogher, 31, 40

Clonmel, 45, 52

Clonoe, 91, 97

Clontibret, battle of, 83

Clifford, Conyers, 84, 86

Cobos, Don Alonso de, 83, 127

Coleraine, 29, 146; county of, 103, 104

Colonies, American, 18, 34, 37, 104, 138; Roman, 35

Colonisation (see Plantation)

Comber, 36

Common Pleas, Court of, 6

Coney island, 31

Congested Districts Board (1891), 118

Connacht, province of, 4, 15, 34, 61–71, 74, 77, 87, 89, 91, 92; composition of, 10, 70–1, 119–121; Presidency of, 49, 64, 65, 84, 101, 117

'Conquistadors' (see Adventurers, Elizabethan)

Conway, Sir Fulke, 104

Copeland islands, 38

Cork, 8, 11, 12, 46, 47, 48, 57, 89, 93; county of, 47, 55, 88, 93, 95, 140

Corrib, river, 62

Corroge, confrontation of, 45

Corunna, 74, 77

'Coshering', 10, 12, 108

Counter-Reformation, 17, 47, 56, 57, 89, 103, 126, 127

de Courcy, John, 36

Courtenay, Thomas, 55, 57

'Coyne & Livery', 10, 12, 108

Crannog (fortified lake dwelling), 39, 82

'Creaght', 9

Cromwell, Oliver, 38

Crown, the (sc. Tudor Monarchy), 4, 6, 15, 16, 17, 18, 19, 20, 23, 25, 37, 41, 45, 50, 60, 62, 68, 70, 79, 101, 102, 103, 104, 108, 114, 116, 126; Union of the Crowns, 17

Cuellar, Don Francisco de, 76–7, 78; his account of the Irish, 109–11

Culloden, battle of, 144

Culmore, fort, 89, 91

Curlew mountains, 70

Currachs (West of Ireland fishing boats), 75

Curraun peninsula, 74

Cushendun, 29, 32, 33

'Cuttings and Spendings', 10, 70, 101, 107, 119

Danzig, 82

Dartmouth, 54

Dartry mountains, 77

Davells, Sir Henry, 55, 56

Davies, Sir John, Attorney General, 20, 101, 104, 111, 122

de Burgo, Richard (Dominus Connaciae), 61

de Burgo, Richard (the 'Red Earl'), 61

de Burgo, Walter (Earl of Ulster), 61

de Burgo, William, 4, 61

de Burgo, William (the 'Brown Earl'), 61

de Burgos, of Connacht, 11, 61

Decies, west Waterford, 11, 45

Dengen (Philipstown), 19, 20

Denny, Lady, 74

'Derbfine' (see Kinship Group)

Derrinlaur castle, 52

Derry, 31, 34, 84, 89, 91, 146; north Derry (O'Cahan's country, later co. Coleraine), 77, 84, 89, 91, 102, 103, 104, 146

Desmond, 16th Earl of, 27, 45, 47, 50–3, 55, 56, 58–9, 69, 70

Desmond, house of, 11, 12, 13, 47, 48, 50, 53, 55, 59, 66, 97, 101, 102, 103, 117

Desmond, Sir James of, 57

Desmond rebellion, 12; first phase, 47–52; second phase, 54–9

Devereux, Penelope (Lady Rich, later Lady Mountjoy), 38

Devon, 46

Dingle, 8, 54, 57; Sovereign of, 73, 93; peninsula, 54, 55, 56, 57

Docwra, Sir Henry, 89, 91, 92, 97

'Dominus Hiberniae' (see Ireland, Lordship of)

Donegal town, 31, 80; abbey, 92, 95; county (see Tyrconnell).

Down, county of, 11, 27, 35, 39, 60, 89, 104; Downshire family (Hills), 104

Drake, Francis, 41, 42, 58, 73

Drogheda, 7, 12, 14, 31, 41, 48, 62, 89

Drury, Sir William, 55

'Dubh-cosh' ('Black rent') 19

Dublin: Archbishop of, 15; castle, 7, 29, 33, 49, 51, 65, 80; city, 6, 7, 8, 28, 50, 51, 62, 80, 81, 86, 87, 89, 96, 97; county, 4, 6; government/administration in, 3, 6, 14, 25, 43, 49, 51, 61, 64, 72, 79, 81; Parliament in, 16, 69–70; foundation of University (1592), 142–3

'Dun-an-Oir' (see Smerwick)

Dunboy castle, 96

Dundalk, 4, 7, 26, 89, 90, 109

Dungannon, 28, 82, 91,

Index

163

Index

Roses, Wars of the, 12
Ross, 8
Rossclogher, castle, 77, 78
Rosses Point, co. Sligo, 76
Route, north Antrim, 11, 28, 29, 37, 68
Russell, Sir William, Lord Deputy (1594-7), 81
Ryan, Dr (Bishop of Killaloe), 57

Saffron Walden, 35
St Leger, Sir Anthony, 23; Sir Warham, 46, 47, 57, 69
St Malo, 52
Saintloo, Edward, 46
Salamanca, 96
Sanders, Dr Nicholas (Papal Nuncio), 56, 125, 129
Savoy, 86, 92; Savoyards, 92
Schoolmen, 88
Scotland, 3, 28, 29, 42, 66, 68, 76, 77, 82; Scots in Antrim, 27, 29, 30, 33, 37, 38, 68, 88; Scots in Connacht, 66-7, 70-1; 'robbers of the Hebrides', 25, 30, 109; Highlanders, 26; influence in Ulster, 28, 29, 68; Scottish intervention in Irish affairs, 46, 61, 66, 67, 70; Mary, Queen of Scots, 102; Scottish masons, 81; Scottish mercenaries, 25 (Redshanks), 27, gallowglasses, 28, 29, 30, 32, 66, 70, 81
Septs, Gaelic, 9, 10, 34, 107
Servitors, 102
Shane's castle, Randalstown, 88
Shanid, 11
Shannon, river and estuary, 8, 19, 51, 52, 56, 61, 64, 66, 73, 95
Shetland islands, 72
Ships: *Achates*, 131; *Anne Aucher*, 54; *Dreadnought*,

67; *Duquesa Santa Anna, La*, 75; *Gran Grin*, 74; *Girona*, 75-6, 130; *Falcon*, 41; *Handmaid*, 67; *Lion*, 67, 87; *Nuestra Senora de Begona, La*, 75; *Rata Coronada, La*, 75; *Revenge*, 73; *San Esteban*, 74; *San Juan*, 73; *San Juan de Ragusa*, 73; *San Juan de Sicilia*, 76; *San Pedro*, 76; *Santa Maria de la Rosa*, 73, 130; *Swiftsure*, 67; *Trinidad*, 74; *Triumph*, 73; *Victory*, 73; *Zuniga*, 74, 76
'Sober ways, politic drifts', 15, 18, 23, 53, 113-14, 136
Soldiers: Aguila's expeditionary force, 92-3; 'Bonaght', 82, 107-8; Bowmen, 38; Cavalry, 82, 84, 86, 89; Essex's expeditionary force, 38; Fitzmaurice's troops, 54-5; Gallowglasses, 28, 30, 82, 107, 108, 109; 'hosting of the Englishry', 30, 68; Infantry, 30, 39, 84, 86, 89, 92; Italian troops, 57-8; Kerne, Irish, 26, 27, 30, 82, 84, 107, 108; Musketeers, 65, 82, 83; Mercenaries, Scots, 27, 28, 29, 30, 32, 50, 70, 81; (redshanks), 25; Irish, 82; O'Neill's cadres, 82; Shane O'Neill's forces, 30-1; Pikemen, 82; Sappers, 58; Surgeons, 38
Southampton, Henry Wriothesley, Earl of, 89
Sidney, Sir Henry (Lord Deputy, 1565-7, 1568-71, 1575-8), 27, 30-4, 40, 43, 45, 47, 48, 64, 65, 66, 69, 71, 79; island Sidney (see Coney island); lough Sidney (see lough Neagh); Sidney, Philip, 66

'Silken Thomas' (see Fitzgerald, Thomas, Lord Offaly)
Slea Head, 54
Sligo, 23; castle, 66, 83, 84, 95; county, 65, 76, 81, 110; town, 31, 78
Smerwick, 54, 55, 57; massacre of, 57-9, 73, 93, 140
Smith, John, 35
Smith, George, 37
Smith, Sir Thomas, 34-7, 36, 43, 45, 53, 60, 79, 103, 145; Thomas (his illegitimate son), 36
Spain, 3, 53, 54, 58, 82, 92, 93, 96; Irish links with, 17; Spaniards (Spanish), 54, 56, 72-8, 93, 95, 96, 138; Spanish Armada, 56, 68, 71, 72-8, 83, 86, 87, 96, 130-1; Aguila at Kinsale, 92-6; Intervention in Irish affairs, 3, 46, 47, 50, 54, 56, 57-8, 61, 82, 83, 86, 89, 109; Spanish officers, 54, 57, 58, 72-8, 82, 93, 95; Spanish Main, 43, 86; Philip II of Spain, 20, 54, 58, 75, 86, 127
Spenser, Edmund, 59, 64, 117, 125-6, 140-1
Stanihurst, Sir James, 142
Stauntons, 61
Sténuit, Robert, 130
Strangford lough, 36
Streedagh strand, 76, 78
Stuarts, 103, 144; Prince Charles Edward, 143
Stukeley, Thomas ('Duke of Ireland'), 54, 57
Subkings (see Urraghts)
Sumptuary regulations, 4, 64, 69
Supremacy, Act of, 16, 17, 69
'Surrender and re-grant', 18, 19, 23, 62, 79, 102, 113
Surrey, Earl of, 18, 113, 136-7
Sussex, Thomas Radcliffe,

Index